Carnivorous Plants

Carnivorous Plants

Tony Camilleri

Photography by Sam Camilleri and Terry Knight
Illustrations by Anna Argent

Kangaroo Press

To Anna
Will you marry me?

First published in Australia in 1998 by Kangaroo Press
an imprint of Simon & Schuster Australia
20 Barcoo Street, East Roseville NSW 2069

A Viacom Company
Sydney New York London Toronto Tokyo Singapore

© Tony Camilleri 1998

National Library of Australia
Cataloguing-in-Publication data

Camilleri, Tony.
Carnivorous plants

Includes bibliographical references.
Includes index.
ISBN 0 86417 917 0.

Internal design: Richard Francis
Illustrator: Anna Argent
Photographers: Sam Camilleri and Terry Knight

Set in Bembo 11/13
Printed in Singapore by Colour Symphony Pte Ltd

10 9 8 7 6 5 4 3 2 1

Cover photograph *Nepenthes maxima*
Photograph opposite previous page *Sarracenia purpurea*

Contents

Acknowledgments

I would like to thank the following people whose valuable assistance and guidance in this project have helped turn this book into a reality:

my brother, Sam, whose patience and persistence have created the majority of the magnificent photographs;

Terry Knight, of Terry Knight and Associates, who provided the valuable extra photographs at very short notice;

Anna Argent, my girlfriend, who provided the diagrams and illustrations;

Dave Wilson for his assistance with the waterwheel plant;

David Rosenberg of Kangaroo Press whose enthusiasm for the book made it all possible;

Sue Read, editor, and Richard Francis, designer, for their expertise;

all the members of the Victorian Carnivorous Plant Society especially Peter Anderson, David Bond and Ron Abernathy who allowed us to photograph their plants.

Special thanks to Colin Clayton at Triffid Park, Collectors Corner Nursery and the staff of the Geelong Botanical Gardens.

Foreword

It was about fifteen years ago that my mother gave me a Venus fly trap, and little could she know that this plant would change the way I look at all plants in the world today. Fascination was the hook; not only could the plant move, but it appeared so bizarre.

What else existed in the world of carnivorous plants?

It didn't take long for me to pursue the answer to that question. The next week I scoured the bookshops to find my first book on carnivorous plants. That book ignited my thirst for knowledge leading me to search out any other book on the subject and leading also to a passion for collecting as many carnivorous plants as possible. Like other enthusiasts whom I know, I developed an intense interest in one genus and it was the tropical pitcher plant (*Nepenthes*) that inspired me the most. Which one will it be for you?

This interest in *Nepenthes* has led me to seek further understanding of the how, what and why of growing that genus. What better way to understand a a group of plants than to find them growing in their natural habitat. I therefore travelled the wild jungles of Borneo, regarded as the central habitat of the genus.

Understanding a plant's requirements in nature is a key factor in successful cultivation at home. Some things you just can't get from books alone. To experience the environment in which a plant grows can be far more rewarding than knowledge gained more conventionally. In travelling to far distant places to see a population of *Nepenthes* in the wild, I've been touched by the people, customs and places I may not have ever dreamed of, if not for my mother's gift of the Venus fly trap.

I hope that this book will inspire you the way I was touched all those years ago. Happy growing!

Peter Anderson
President
Victorian Carnivorous Plant Society

A small fly has just been caught in the sticky tentacles of a sundew plant.

Preface

Charles Darwin, the author of *The Origin of Species* and the theory of evolution was so fascinated by carnivorous plants which glistened in the sunlight and captured insects around the Sussex countryside that he could not resist taking some plants home with him.

The idea that a plant could not only capture insects but also devour them for food led his curious mind to begin exhaustive tests on these plants.

His wife Emma was grateful to the sundew in that it gave relief to her husband from many of his concerns in writing the *Origin of Species*. In a letter she wrote: 'Charles is too much given to anxiety, as you know, and his various experiments this summer have been a great blessing to him. At present he is treating *Drosera* just like a living creature, and I suppose he hopes to end in proving it an animal'.

Darwin's experiments continued for fifteen years and resulted in his *Insectivorous Plants* published in 1875 in which he remarked that the Venus fly trap was 'the most wonderful plant in the world'.

The term 'carnivorous plant' was first applied during 1760 by Governor Dobbs of North Carolina in the United States of America. He was referring to the Venus fly trap, which is native to that region. At that time, little was known about the variety of carnivorous plants growing around the world, with many people believing that the Venus fly trap was the only plant of its kind.

This could not be further from the truth, and we now know of 500 different species in many varied habitats, all fascinating in their own way with their own methods of capturing insects. The unusual characteristics and often spectacular appearance of these plants has created an unprecedented interest in growing carnivorous plants. It is now common to find them on sale at your local supermarket.

However, the increase in popularity of some species has resulted in catastrophic effects to their populations. It is estimated that in 1990, more than two million Venus fly traps were collected in the wild. Of the 21 counties in the states of North and South Carolina in the United States of America which were originally home to these plants, only 11 can still claim this distinction.

The pitcher and tropical pitcher plants are suffering the same fate, with their habitats being removed to build farms. The state of North Carolina now imposes fines of up to US$2000 for the illegal removal of the plant and the Convention on International Trade of Endangered Species (CITES) also offers special protection.

Specialised nurseries and societies have now established themselves trading in the many varieties of carnivorous plants. Most plants are available from these nurseries, many of which provide a mail order service. Most of these nurseries grow their plants using tissue culture. For details of these outlets, refer to Appendix B.

In this book I have attempted to capture the beauty, colour and shapes of these spectacular plants. Included are many of the different species available in cultivation. The book is intended as a layperson's guide to the understanding and appreciation of the growth and habits of meat-eating plants. The structure of the book is such that each chapter's material is further amplified by a comprehensive listing in the appendix providing details on basic growth characteristics of each species. It is my hope that whether you are an avid beginner or an experienced grower, you will find this publication interesting, practical and thought-provoking.

Opposite Tropic pitcher plant *Nepenthes maxima*, lower pitcher

Introduction

What is a carnivorous plant?

The definition of a carnivorous plant is simply any plant which has adapted to supplement its diet by capturing and digesting insects.

There are about 560 different individual species distributed worldwide which can be categorised into 20 separate genera. It must be stressed that 'carnivorous plant' is a generic term only and many species are totally unrelated. Due to the relatively new interest in these plants, and because of their sometimes highly inaccessible native terrain and the minute size of some plants, new species of carnivorous plants continue to be discovered every year.

The climatic conditions in which they grow vary from the extreme conditions of tropical rainforest to snow-capped mountains with torrential rainfalls. The most essential ingredient for all carnivorous plants is the abundance of water.

Why do they devour insects?

Carnivorous plants generally grow and thrive in conditions in which many other plants cannot survive. These areas are usually swampy and extremely boggy, and receive an abundance of water. The soils in these areas are poor and deficient of any nutrition.

This nutrition deficiency has enabled carnivorous plants to develop a unique method of supplementing their diet. Their solution is the ability to devour insects in order to obtain nutrition. All carnivorous plants have the ability to extract the goodness from insects by firstly capturing them through a variety of ingenious methods and then dissolving them with digestive juices and enzymes which they release after capturing their prey.

Contrary to popular belief, it is not necessary to feed insects to your plant. An abundance or over-feeding with insects will actually harm or even kill a plant. An ingestion of insects to a carnivorous plant is like a fertiliser boost for any other plant. The most practical suggestion is to allow your plant to capture insects naturally.

Above Sundew (*Drosera* spp.)
Opposite Sun pitcher (*Heliamphora* spp.)
Below Venus fly trap (*Dionaea muscipula*)

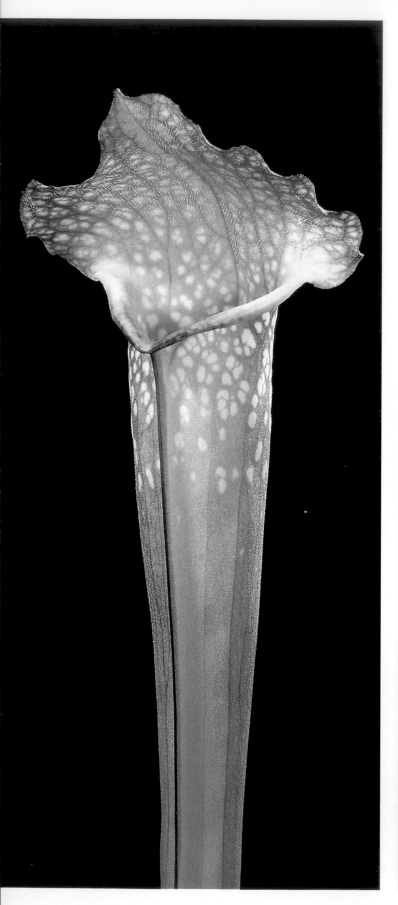

Types of traps

There are two insect trapping mechanisms; all carnivorous plants are categorised according to which of the two they possess:

• passive traps—traps which do not move and rely on the insect to be lured into or onto the digestive system;

• active traps—traps which move and enclose their prey.

Left Pitcher plant

Below Tropical pitcher plant hybrid
Nepenthes maxima x veitchii

How did carnivorous plants evolve?

Many carnivorous plant genera are totally unrelated and therefore would have had their own separate evolutionary background. There have not been any fossilised remains of carnivorous plants therefore scientific evidence of their evolution is minimal. However there are a few clues which have generated some theories.

Two species which offer clues to their evolution are the *Heliamphora* and *Triphyophyllum*.

Heliamphora is the most primitive in appearance and is thought to be the missing link between non-carnivorous and carnivorous plants. Its shape clearly resembles a leaf which has folded and merged to become a pitcher.

It survives exclusively on the huge sandstone mountain plateau tops of Venezuela in South America. Geological evidence suggests these mountains were isolated from the surrounding areas about 1600 million years ago. It is believed that *Heliamphora* needed to adapt to a changing climate of continuous rainfall and the removal of nutrition from the soil surface by the water cascading from the mountain. The suggestion is that the evolutionary process created a species of plant with the ability to capture insects because of the need to supplement its diet.

The *Triphyophyllum* is an unusual and very rare species which is a tropical woody climber native to the rain forests of Sierra Leone, Liberia and the Ivory Coast in Western Africa. This species is unusual in that it produces three distinctly different types of leaves that correlate with separate phases of growth. The early growth produces slender and lance-shaped leaves. The second stage of growth produces carnivorous gland-like leaves, similar to a sundew. Two years after reaching maturity, the third stage produces leaves with tendrils at the tip to enable it to climb. The *Triphyophyllum* has been scientifically linked to the sundew and tropical pitcher plant in that its structure is similar to these two genera.

Therefore, this species with its change from carnivorous to non-carnivorous state offers clues to studies of carnivorous plants and their evolution. At some time every species had to change form in a similar fashion.

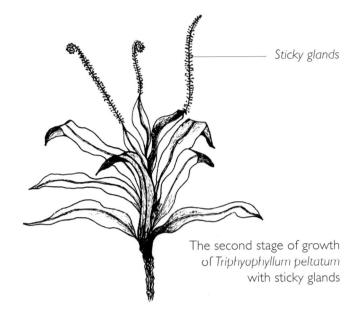

Sticky glands

The second stage of growth of *Triphyophyllum peltatum* with sticky glands

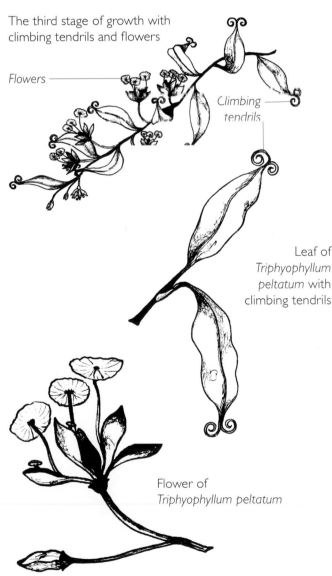

The third stage of growth with climbing tendrils and flowers

Flowers

Climbing tendrils

Leaf of *Triphyophyllum peltatum* with climbing tendrils

Flower of *Triphyophyllum peltatum*

1

Venus fly trap

Family: Droseraceae
Botanical name: *Dionaea muscipula*
Distribution: See map.

By far the most popular and easiest to recognise of all carnivorous plant species, the Venus fly trap is often an enthusiast's first introduction into the fascinating world of meat-eating plants. Many begin their interest with the purchase of this species growing in a little pot by the windowsill. Charles Darwin described it as 'one of the most wonderful plants in the world'.

With an understanding of the fascinating methods this plant has developed to capture insects, it is easy to marvel at its amazing capabilities.

Capturing insects

The Venus fly trap possesses the uncanny and fascinating capability of movement to capture its food. Insects are lured into the deadly, bright red trap of the sweet-smelling, sweet-tasting nectar exuded by the plant. Once an insect has strayed into the awaiting trap it suckles on the abundance of food. Little does the victim realise, that the slightest touch of the tiny hairs within the trap will trigger a sudden shutting motion.

Opposite Venus fly trap—red variety

The open trap is ready and waiting for its prey. The red colour and sweet-smelling nectar entice the insect to enter the trap.

A fly has been captured and the trap instantly closes.

After a few days, the trap re-opens to reveal the shell of a decayed fly.

CANADA

UNITED STATES OF AMERICA

North Carolina

South Carolina

MEXICO

Above A comparison of a conventional sized trap and the 'big mouth' variety which produces large traps on very short leaves

Above Venus fly trap variety with sawtooth edge rather than fine pointed hairs

Below Akai Ryu 'Red Dragon' produces red leaves and traps. Developed by Atlanta Botanical Gardens in the USA.

Within moments the trap closes, imprisoning its victim. However, in the first instance, the trap will only three-quarters close, allowing any small insects to escape through the gap between the little fingers on the outside of the trap. An appropriately sized meal has no chance of release. Within hours, the trap will slowly tighten shut and squeeze the insect. Once the trap is fully closed, the plant releases its digestive acids and enzymes which slowly break down and devour the insect. The nutritious meal is then absorbed into the plant. After a few days the trap will re-open to reveal the empty shell of an insect; the Venus fly trap is now ready for its next victim. Each single trap will open and close only a few times in its lifetime, after which it will blacken and die.

Whilst there is only one species of Venus fly trap, there are many varieties.

The plant

The Venus fly trap grows from a rhizome, which is basically a name for a plant stem which is beneath the surface of the soil. A good healthy plant generally produces about six traps or leaves. The normal growing cycle of a plant involves traps which develop and then blacken and die. Once a trap has blackened, it is best to cut it off in order to allow a new trap to grow in its place. New traps are quickly reproduced.

During early spring, a flower stem, called a scape breaks through the soil and grows up the centre of the rosette. This stem can grow up to 30 cm (12 in) high. Once the stem is fully grown, small white flowers will burst open.

Dormancy

During winter, the plant ceases growing and enters a dormancy period. The onset of the cold weather usually triggers this phase.

Dormancy is necessary as it is the normal growing cycle of this and many other species of carnivorous plants. Specimens which do not become dormant will die within a few years.

Plants living in tropical and warmer climates will not naturally enter a dormancy period due to the lack of cold weather. In this instance, it is recommended to remove the plant from its pot, cut all leaves and wrap the living rhizome in moist sphagnum moss and plastic and then place it into the refrigerator for three months to induce dormancy.

After three months the rhizome can then be re-potted and new leaves will appear within a few weeks.

Venus fly trap

Keeping and caring for your plant

The Venus fly trap can make an interesting and enjoyable house plant. To ensure long life of your plant, you should be aware of the following growing conditions.

POTTING MEDIUM A good all-purpose potting mixture is three parts peat moss and one part coarse river sand or vermiculite (all obtainable from your local nursery). The peat moss acts as a nutrient deficient soil, whilst the sand or vermiculite assists the drainage and aerates the soil. Remembering that carnivorous plants obtain their nutrition from capturing insects, another recommended addition to the mixture is chopped live sphagnum moss which will grow as a green cover on the surface. This will act as an excellent moisture indicator. If the sphagnum moss begins to turn brown, the soil is lacking water.

LIGHT A healthy specimen should be kept in full sun within temperate climates. The plant can tolerate temperatures of up to 35° Celsius (95° Fahrenheit) in the sun. This will enable an attractive redness to appear within the trap.

WATERING The Venus fly trap grows natively in boggy areas. It therefore requires to be kept in constant supply of water . The pot should be kept in a water tray with about 2 cm (1 in) of water at all times. The roots will absorb the water from below and keep them continually moist. The plant ideally requires distilled or rain water.

Continual use of normal tap water could cause a build up of salt and therefore shorten the lifespan (depending on quality of water in your area). If distilled or rain water is difficult to obtain, it is recommended to allow the tap water to stand for a few days in a container out in the sun. Alternatively, boil the water and allow it to cool. Both methods will break down the salt. If tap water is continually used, it is advisable to re-pot the plant annually into a fresh potting mixture.

The flowers

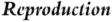

Above Rhizome and roots

Opposite The flower stem grows out of the clump of traps in early spring.

Reproduction

The Venus fly trap has a number of methods which enable it to reproduce.

SEEDS Seeds can be collected from your plant after flowering. Once a plant has flowered and pollination occurs, it will fertilise the ovules (unfertilised seeds). The ovules are contained within the ovary. Once fertilisation occurs, the ovary enlarges and after six to eight weeks it turns black and the seeds ripen.

Alternatively, seeds can be obtained from specialised carnivorous plant growers and societies. Some of these are listed in Appendix A.

Once seed is obtained, it can be sown on a medium of 80% peat and 20% sand in seed trays during early spring. The tray is to stand in water with full light. The seeds sprout in about two weeks to a month. The first growth that develops is unlike the regular leaves and is referred to as the seed leaves. The next growth contains tiny new traps which are like adult plants in every respect.

RHIZOME SPLITTING The Venus fly trap has the ability to reproduce through the natural cycle of rhizome multiplying. Generally, a healthy plant consists of about six traps. If more than six are present, it is likely that the rhizome has multiplied. The plant can then be dug out and the rhizome separated to create two or more plants.

RHIZOME CUTTING A new plant can be produced by the method of taking a cutting. The outermost leaves can be removed, ensuring that a little of the rhizome is also taken. The leaf is then placed partly inside moist sphagnum moss. After a few days, the part of the leaf out of the sphagnum will die. However, the portion within the sphagnum moss will produce roots and begin to grow.

Problem solving

The traps will grow but will not open.	You may be using fertiliser or a regular potting mix which contains nutrients. This will signal to the plant that it is not necessary to capture insects to obtain nutrition.
The traps have long thin leaves and remain green.	This indicates a deficiency of sunlight. Four hours of sunlight per day is recommended. With the introduction of sunlight, redness and stronger new growth should appear within a month.

2

Sundew

Family: Droseraceae

Botanical name: *Drosera* (from the Greek *droseros*, dewy)

Distribution: See map.

The sundew derives its name from the glorious effect it displays glistening in the sun when its sticky tentacles are wet. The tiny glue-like tentacles protrude from the edge of the leaf; these tentacles then form droplets of a sticky substance which in turn is used to capture prey.

When the insect lands on the tentacle, it is instantly glued onto the plant. Within minutes the sundew slowly closes around the insect and further tightens its grip on the prey. The more the insect struggles the stronger it is held by its glue. Enzymes are then slowly released from the plant's tentacles breaking down the protein from the insect which is then absorbed by the leaf.

In his book *Insectivorous Plants* which was published in 1875, Charles Darwin observed that the minutest particle would trigger the plant. With respect to its sensitivity, he stated: 'It was doubtful that a single nerve in the human body could have detected or been affected by so minute a particle. It appears to me that hardly any

Opposite A new flower stem shooting up from a sundew

Above A fly has no chance of escape once it lands on the sticky tentacles of a *Drosera binata*.

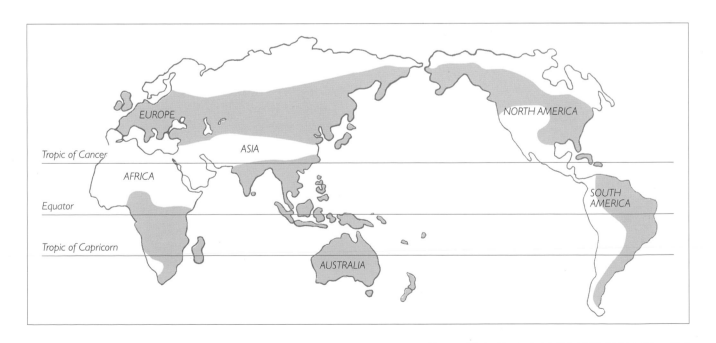

Above Erect sundew—a new leaf unfurling from a *Drosera filiformis*

Below When the tentacles are wet, the tiny droplets glisten brightly in the light. Seen here is a *Drosera binata*.

more remarkable fact has been observed in the vegetable kingdom'. Another discovery documented by Darwin regarding the sundew's digestive juices was that: 'the *Drosera* digested insects by exactly the same process as the animal stomach did meat. What was more, the digestive secretions were remarkably similar'. Darwin concluded:'That a plant and an animal should pour forth the same or nearly the same complex secretion is a new and wonderful fact in physiology'.

There are over 180 species of sundews distributed around the world. In Australia there are about 66 named species with about 53 situated in the south-west of Western Australia. Distribution of the plant occurs mainly in temperate and tropical conditions.

Keeping and caring for your plant

Sundews grow in a variety of habitats and climates. Their organisation into the following categories indicates which species will suit your particular climate. Check the listing in the back of the book to find to which category each species belongs.

- Temperate species (non-tuberous)
- Tuberous species
- Pygmy sundews
- Tropical species
- Sub-tropical species

Physical Appearance

The sundew appears in a variety of forms:

Rosetted sundews. Rosetted sundews possess a basal rosette of leaves. The leaf stalks can scarcely be distinguished from the leaf blade. They are generally larger bulbous-rooted plants, many of which are tuberous.

Fan-leaved sundews. These sundews have a basal rosette with one or more erect leafy stems. The leaf blade is usually fan-shaped.

Pygmy sundews. The pygmy sundew is a species distinguished by its miniature size. There are about 17 species, all of which are native to Australia.

Erect sundews. This is a group with tall, long narrow leaves.

Scrambling sundews. The scrambling sundew is similar in appearance to an erect sundew but its weak root structure usually does not allow the plant to grow tall. Rather it scrambles along the surface of the ground.

Climbing sundews. Slender plants with the ability to climb.

Above *Drosera alciae* is a typical example of a rosetted sundew.

Right Close-up of sticky globules

The temperate species (non-tuberous)

The majority of species in this group are from South Africa and southern Australia. Most are rather hardy, easy to keep and can produce beautiful flowers in the spring. Species like *Drosera capensis* and *D. binata* have been described as growing like weeds.

POTTING MIX A general mix of three parts peat moss to one part sand is usually adequate.

LIGHT Most should be kept in a bright filtered sunlight position.

WATERING Keeping the plants in a tray of water is most suitable for this group. Remember to reduce the quantity of water during the winter.

The tuberous species

Tuberous sundews are currently unique to Australia. These sundews grow only during winter and die down during summer to exist as a tuber underground. This underground bud enables the plant to survive during the drier months through the storage of food reserves.

When autumn approaches, the renewed growth produces a tiny stem which grows upward from the tuber and when it reaches the soil surface it produces the plant. It is important that the tiny upward stem is not disturbed. If disturbed, the tuber should be placed close to the soil surface. The plant will eventually find its own level again.

New tubers will be produced every year to replace the old tuber. Some species produce more than one tuber that assists in the reproduction. When the new growth occurs, it relies entirely on the nutrition in the tuber until new roots and leaves are produced.

POTTING MIX These species grow natively in sandy soils. A recommended mix is two parts sand to one part peat moss.

LIGHT Filtered light is appropriate

WATERING In summer keep plant moist. Do not over water as the tuber may rot. In the winter growing period, water regularly from above. Do not stand in a container of water altough a minority of species can tolerate it e.g. *D. gigantea*, *D. peltata* and *D. whittakeri*.

POTS They require deep pots due to the long dropper stem which is produced.

Top *Drosera whittakeri*, tuberous sundew

Left *Drosera glabripes* with flower from South African temperate climate

Above *Drosera peltata* has the ability to attach itself to branches and climb.

Left *Drosera peltata* growing in its native habitat

Below A rosetted sundew, *Drosera slackii*

Above Pygmy sundew, *Drosera nitidula* x *ericksoniae*, in flower

Below Pygmy sundew, *Drosera dichrosepala*, measures only about 6 mm across.

Pygmy sundews

All of these species, except for one, grow in the temperate climate of Western Australia. The pygmy sundews are rather hardy, very drought-resistant and can easily survive a long hot summer.

The pygmy sundew has a unique and most fascinating method of reproduction. As the winter months approach, the plants produce additional small vegetative non-sexual parts called gemmae. Each gemma forms in the centre of the rosette and is living. When it forms, it is important that a suitable growing environment is found quickly otherwise it will die. When the autumn rains arrive, they splash the gemmae onto the ground, which in turn allows the growth process to begin. A mature plant can be produced from gemmae within twelve months.

POTTING MIX   A generally easy group to keep, the pygmy sundews require a relatively sandy potting mix about one part peat moss to one part sand.

LIGHT   A filtered light position is generally suitable.

WATERING   They are best stood in water during summer and kept moist during winter.

Propagation

The pygmy sundew can be propagated by the usual method of collecting seed from its flowers. Otherwise, the gemmae can simply be flicked from the plant and placed on the surface of the same pot. Each gemma will soon then produce leaves and roots to form an exact replica of the parent plant.

The pygmy sundew will quickly spread across a pot or terrarium as it multiplies by gemmae and seed dispersal.

The tropical and sub-tropical species

The majority of species in this group are from northern Australia, South America and Central Africa. They generally grow in a climate of continuous warmth and humidity.

This group is recommended for warmer climates only, otherwise they must be grown in a terrarium or hothouse. Many of them cannot tolerate temperatures below 10° Celsius (50° Fahrenheit).

My experience with the northern Australian species is that they must be kept wet in summer and allowed to dry out in winter. Many of these species experience a dormancy during winter, with the entire plant drying out above the surface and surviving only underground, similar to a tuberous sundew.

The environment in which a tropical species will survive includes the dry and wet seasons. The dry season being warm and totally deficient of any rainfall for five months is the dormancy period for tropical sundews. The wet season brings the onset of near-continuous rainfall and humidity between 70% and 95%; this is their growing period.

Unless these conditions can be simulated it can be difficult to keep this group for long periods of time.

POTTING MIX A sandy mix is required with about 50% sand and 50% peat moss. Some species will grow in straight sphagnum moss which maintains a high humidity level for the plant.

WATERING Keep pot in a tray of water during summer. Keep pot only moist during winter, removing it from the tray.

Above Drosera burmanii (Photo: Terry Knight)

Below Tropical sundew, the recently named *Drosera darwinensis* (Photo: Terry Knight)

Below Drosera indica (Photo: Terry Knight)

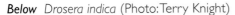

Below Tropical sundew, *Drosera petiolaris* (Photo: Terry Knight)

3

Rainbow plant

Family: Byblidaceae
Botanical name: *Byblis*
Distribution: See map.

In Greek mythology, Byblis was the daughter of Miletus, who was the son of Apollo, the most revered and influential of all Greek gods. She fell in love with her twin brother, but her love was not returned by him and he fled. Her subsequent sorrowful tears caused Byblis to be transformed into a fountain.

The watery droplets of the fountain are the basis of the rainbow plant's name.

The genus *Byblis* is found in Australia and Papua New Guinea. It was formerly known as having only two species, but was recently revised into five species. These plants can be easily mistaken as belonging to the sundew genus since they are similar in appearance to an erect sundew.

However, one distinct difference enables them to be placed into their own genus. Unlike sundews, these species do not possess any ability to move enabling them to close around their prey.

The rainbow plants prefer to be kept in sub-tropical to tropical climates with warmth all year round. Growers in cooler climates have experienced difficulty in keeping these species for an extended period of time. The plants often die in the winter months.

Capturing prey

Otherwise known as a passive flypaper trap, the rainbow plant captures its prey in a very similar method to a sundew, with the insect becoming glued onto the plant after landing into its sticky tentacles. Once an insect is captured, the digestive glands slowly release their enzymes and the insect is consumed.

All species are extremely efficient at capturing small insects and one plant can have as many as twenty bugs lodged on it at one time.

Opposite *Byblis gigantea* (Photo: Terry Knight)

Byblis gigantea
Distribution: Western Australia

The largest of the species, *Byblis gigantea*, grows up to 60 cm (2 ft) in height. Long, vertically erect stems are produced with sticky glandular hairs throughout. The plant lies dormant throughout summer, until new growth appears with the first rains of winter. It flowers usually in spring when numerous purple or lilac flowers appear.

Keeping and caring for your plant

POTTING MIX This species requires to be kept in a very open sandy mixture of about one part sand or vermiculite to one part peat moss. A deep pot is necessary to allow the long roots to develop.

Propagation

SEED This is a difficult species to germinate from seed. Within its native habitat, new growth appears a few weeks after a fire has ravaged the area. Therefore, seeds will generally only germinate after the simulation of a fire has occurred.

Sow the seeds about 4 cm (1.5 in) within the soil mix and place many dry gum leaves on the surface. Set the leaves alight and allow them to burn out. Germination should occur within a month.

Byblis gigantea (Photo: Terry Knight)

Byblis aquatica (Photo: Terry Knight)

Byblis liniflora

Distribution: Northern Australia and Papua New Guinea

This is a slender, rather weak plant growing to 15 cm (6 in) in length which can often be found in high well drained soils, straggling along the ground amongst the tall grass during the wet season in northern Australia and Papua New Guinea (October to May).

An annual in its native habitat, *B. liniflora* dies off during the tropical dry season of northern Australia (May–Sept). Several flowers, pinkish mauve with white underside, are continuously opening during its growing season and produce an abundance of seeds. It usually flowers from December to April.

Keeping and caring for your plant

POTTING MIX The standard soil mix of two parts peat moss to one part sand is adequate with the pot allowed to sit in a saucer of water during summer. During winter, remove the pot from the water and allow the soil to be kept moist, but not wet.

LIGHT AND TEMPERATURE *Byblis liniflora* flourishes in a warm and humid climate with filtered sunlight. It will grow alongside *Nepenthes* in a hothouse. The temperature should be maintained between 15°–30° Celsius (59°–86° Fahrenheit).

My experience with this species is that the *liniflora* will usually drop an abundance of seed and multiply rapidly over a period of a few years if kept in the correct conditions.

Propagation

SEED The seed can be easily collected and sown during early spring. Humidity, which assists germination, can be increased by covering the pot with plastic. Germination will usually occur within about two weeks.

Byblis aquatica

Distribution: Northern Territory, Australia

Usually found growing near *B. liniflora*, however generally in shallow depressions and beside freshwater lagoons. The stem can grow up to 45 cm (18 in) in length, however only about 5 cm (2 in) is obvious, with the remainder straggling or floating. This species is often flooded during the wetter times of the year.

The species flowers between January and May and is purple in colour.

Byblis filifolia

Distribution: Western Australia and Northern Territory

Growing up to 60 cm (2 feet) in length, the stem of this species is erect or leans against surrounding vegetation. The flowers are mauve on the upperside and white, yellow, or yellow with mauve stripes on the underside. It flowers from March to June.

Byblis rorida

Distribution: Western Australia

Growing to 6 to 30 cm (2 to 12 in) in length, this species is found mainly beside creeks and lakes. Flowers are mauve on the upperside and white on the underside.

4

Waterwheel plant

Family: Droseraceae
Botanical name: *Aldrovanda vesiculosa*
Distribution: See map

An aquatic species and the only one of its genus, *Aldrovanda vesiculosa* is a small plant surviving between the reeds in acidic swamps and lakes. Whilst it is recorded as being widely distributed in Europe, Africa, Japan, India and Australia, the reality is that it is an endangered species in Poland, Switzerland and rare in Bulgaria, China, Croatia, the Czech Republic, Hungary and Russia. The species is now extinct in Japan, Bangladesh, Denmark, France, Germany, Italy and Japan.

A single stem appears under the surface of the water. Generally eight leaves or traps grow in a circular shape around the stem at small intervals. The stem seldom exceeds 15 cm (6 in) in length. As new growth appears, the old stem dies off. Like most aquatic species, the plant is rootless.

This species has the ability to capture mosquito larvae, small spiders and any other tiny swimming insects.

Single white flowers appear in summer just above the water surface on a short stem.

Opposite The waterwheel plant (Photo: Terry Knight)

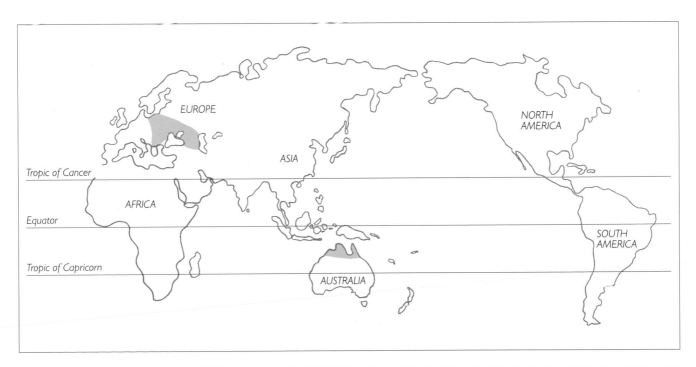

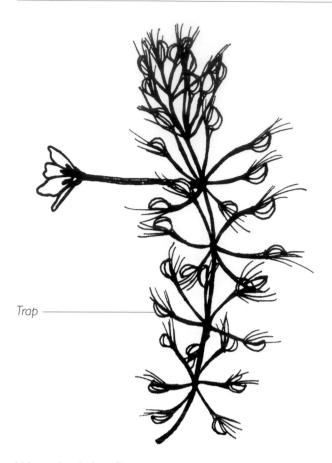

Trap ─────────

Waterwheel plant flower

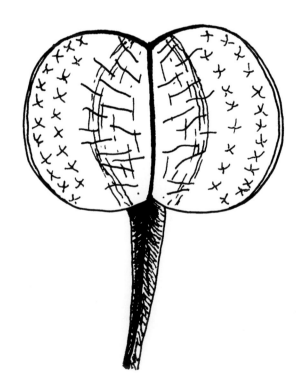

Close-up of trap

Capturing prey

Whilst only measuring about 2 mm in length, the trapping mechanism can be compared to the Venus fly trap. The awaiting trap is made up of two lobes which are open and ready to capture prey. Tiny trigger hairs, which number about forty, cause the trap to snap shut once they're touched.

The closing movement is quick and takes about one fiftieth of a second, giving little chance for the victim to escape. Once the trap is closed, it begins a narrowing phase and slowly squeezes tightly shut, releasing excess water in the process.

When the trap has fully closed, digestive acids are released and the prey is slowly digested.

Keeping and caring for your plant

This species can be difficult to cultivate and has exact requirements, otherwise it will rapidly deteriorate and die. Therefore, it is only recommended to the dedicated grower.

WATER Like an aquatic bladderwort, the waterwheel plant needs to be kept in a container of acidic water. This is achieved through placing a layer of peat on the bottom, filling with water and allowing it to settle for a few days. The floating layer should be removed before the plant is placed in the container.

The acid level should be high enough so that the water colour is yellow. The resulting pH level would be between 5 and 6. A simple pH test kit which is available at an aquarium can be used to measure pH level. Adding or reducing peat will vary the level of pH.

The waterwheel plant is assisted in its growth through the addition of a layer of decomposing leaves and other aquatic grasses which assist in keeping the pH level low and lowering nutrient level in the water.

LIGHT Keep the container out of direct sunlight, as algae could form. Algae will quickly destroy the plant.

TEMPERATURE The water temperature needs to be maintained at between 20°–30° Celsius (68°–86° Fahrenheit).

Carbon dioxide reactor

An ingredient which has been found extremely helpful in the care of the waterwheel plant is carbon dioxide, which appears to dramatically increase its growth rate.

A simple carbon dioxide reactor can be made with the following equipment:
• a 5 litre container
• 250 grams sugar
• one teaspoon yeast

Fill the container with three litres of water and 250 grams sugar. Add one teaspoon of yeast and stir. Seal the top and allow carbon dioxide to be released through a hose from the bottle into a small plastic soft drink container cut in half. This smaller container acts as a carbon dioxide diffuser which disperses the gas into the water holding the waterwheel plant. This setup needs to be replaced every two weeks as the yeast will gradually cease to produce carbon dioxide.

Above Waterwheel plant seen from above water surface

Above left Typical habitat of the waterwheel plant in northern Australia

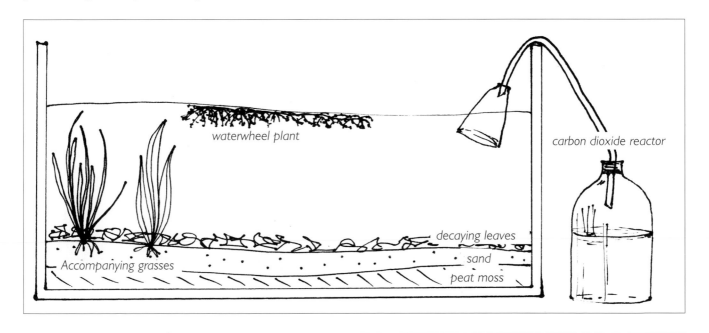

waterwheel plant

carbon dioxide reactor

decaying leaves

sand

peat moss

Accompanying grasses

5

Pitcher plant

Family: Sarraceniaceae
Botanical name: *Sarracenia*
Distribution: USA. See map.

The pitcher plant is a very popular and attractive genus of carnivorous plant which is easy to grow in most temperate climates. So impressive are some of the pitchers that they are widely used in floral displays around the United States and Europe. It has been estimated that the market for cut pitchers is in the millions. It is a genus otherwise known as trumpet pitchers and grows natively, mainly in the south-east of the United States.

The pitcher plant derives its name from the shape of the plant which is basically a leaf that has moulded itself to take the form of a funnel.

Another fascinating aspect of this genus is the unusual flower which grows annually from a tall stem that shoots up from the surface. The unusual and often beautifully coloured flower stands erect in a nodding position.

Within the *Sarracenia* genus, there are eight species which can be categorised into two distinct groups:

Prostrate plants. In this group, the pitchers lie along the ground in a horizontal position (*S. purpurea* and *S. psittacina*);

Upright plants. In this group the pitchers grow vertically to heights of up to a metre (three feet) tall.

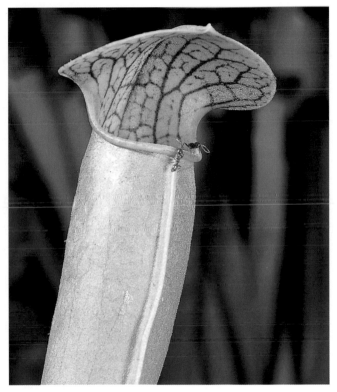

Above An ant suckles on the sweet tasting nectar on the rim of the pitcher.

Opposite *Sarracenia flava*

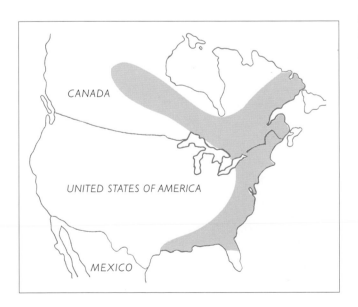

CANADA

UNITED STATES OF AMERICA

MEXICO

Above The long downward-pointing hairs cause any insect to lose its footing and fall inside the pitcher.

Below Insects quickly drown and are absorbed as food for the plant.

Trapping insects

Being a passive carnivore, the pitcher plant must first entice insects into its pitcher, and create mechanisms which make it very difficult for the prey to escape once inside. Each plant in this genus has slightly different adaptions to capturing prey. However, the concept is similar in each plant.

The *Sarracenia* is made up of a pitcher with a hood above it. Externally, the pitcher plant has nectar glands which attract insects. These nectar glands secrete sweet-tasting nectar and are most abundant at the top of the pitcher and the entrance of the mouth.

Once inside, an insect quickly loses its footing on the slippery surface and falls into the potent brew of digestive enzymes at the base of the pitcher. Escape is very difficult at this stage, as long downward-pointing hairs above the liquid make it extremely difficult for an insect to climb out. The insect is then slowly digested and dissolved to become a nutritious meal for the pitcher plant.

Sarracenia alata

Common name: pale pitcher plant
Different forms: green
                red throat
                pubescens
Distribution: eastern Texas, south Louisiana, south
          Mississippi, south-west Alabama, USA

These are tall pitchers which grow about 60 cm (24 in) in height. Generally, they are pale green when young and later become light green with vertical red veins. The red throat form becomes deep burgundy within the pitcher.

Flower is pale yellow to creamy-white.

Sarracenia flava

Common name: yellow trumpet
Distribution: south Alabama, north Florida, south
          Georgia, Carolina, south-west Virginia, USA.
Variations: *maxima*—wholly green from Carolina's
              coastal plain.
              ornata—heavily veined
              copper lid
              Marston Dwarf
              red

Pitchers are tall and erect usually 50–75 cm (20–30 in) in height, depending on which variation. Pitchers can grow up to 1 m (39 in). Colour variations include green, greenish-yellow, bright yellow and red. Hood is distinctive in that it curls up as it meets the pitcher.

Flowers are the largest in the *Sarracenia* genus with yellow petals.

Sarracenia leucophylla

Common name: white trumpet
Distribution: north-west Florida, south-west
          Georgia, south Alabama, USA.
Variations: short pitcher, deep red veins
             green veins, yellow flower

These are very tall pitchers which can grow up to 1 m (39 in) in height. This particular species is very popular in the cut pitcher market. The pitcher is generally green with the top section flaring out and changing colour. White is the dominant colour with either green or red veins.

Flowers grow from a single stem and are either deep red or yellow.

Above Sarracenia alata

Below Sarracenia leucophylla

Sarracenia oreophila

Common name: green pitcher plant
Distribution: north-east Alabama, USA
Variation: heavily veined

Similar in appearance to the *S. flava* with pitchers growing up to 60 cm (24 in). The pitchers are generally green with red veins that can become entirely red in full sunlight.

One distinguishing feature is the non-carnivorous leaves called phyllodia which appear on mature plants during winter. The pitchers die off during this period. The flowers of the *S. oreophila* are yellowish green.

Sarracenia minor

Common name: hooded pitcher plant
Distribution: North and South Carolina, Georgia,
    Florida, USA
Variation: Okefenokee giant

Vertical pitchers grow up to about 60 cm (24 in) however the Okefenokee giant has been known to grow up to twice the size. Green in colour, however looks a brownish red colour when exposed to sunlight. Hood is dispersed with red veins. Ingenious trapping method which consists of windows or areolae on the back of the pitcher. Areolae are supported with a large hood that blocks light to the pitcher.

Once insects are attracted to the mouth of the pitcher they are enticed to leave through the areolae which gives the impression of a clear exit due to the transparency of the window. Insects then fall inside pitcher when attempting to exit.

Yellow flowers appear on a stem which grows below the height of the pitcher.

Top right *Sarracenia minor*

Right Close-up of *Sarracenia minor* showing windows or areole at rear of pitcher

Opposite *Sarracenia oreophilla*

Sarracenia psittacina

Common name: parrot pitcher
Distribution: south Georgia, north Florida, south
Mississippi, Louisiana, USA

A prostrate plant with pitchers that grow up to 25 cm (10 in) in length. A mature pitcher which has been given ample sunlight will be a burgundy in colour with patches of white. Otherwise it may remain green.

A very distinctive looking plant as its name originates from the resemblance a mature pitcher has with a parrot's beak. The head of the pitcher is fully enclosed and bulbous, with a small entrance at the base of the head for its prey. The parrot pitcher is assisted by windows or areolae to capture insects, similar to *S. minor*. Whilst the small entrance to the pitcher is not a very efficient trapping mechanism, it is believed that this species may have developed to suit its native environment. This plant is found in areas that are regularly prone to flooding. The parrot pitcher has developed to become an effective captor of aquatic species who swim into its small entrance and cannot escape. The small red flowers grow on 25 cm (10 in) scapes.

Sarracenia purpurea

Common name: purple pitcher plant
Distribution: eastern USA, Canada. See map.
Sub-species: *purpurea—typica* and *heterophylla*
venosa—typica (chipola and small leaf)
burkii

A prostrate plant which is the most wide ranging in the *Sarracenia* genus.
There are two sub-species of *S. purpurea*:

S. purpurea ssp. *purpurea* (northern pitcher plant) has green pitchers which grow in a rosette around the rhizome. Flowers are red.

S. purpurea ssp. *venosa* (southern pitcher plant) is the more attractive of the two and grows burgundy pitchers with larger hoods. Microscopic white hairs grow only on this sup-species. Flowers are pink or red.

Top *Sarracenia psittacina* with new pitchers forming

Centre *Sarracenia purpurea*

Left *Sarracenia purpurea* ssp. *venosa*

Sarracenia rubra

Common name: sweet trumpet
Distribution: Georgia, South Carolina, Alabama, USA
Sub-species: *rubra*
           alabamensis (typical, red)
           gulfensis
           jonessi (red, green)
           wherryi

Erect pitchers with a fairly narrow tube that gradually widen at the mouth. The hood is quite large and can grow up to twice the width of the tube.

ssp. *rubra*:
Pitcher height: 15–40 cm (6–16 in).
Colours: green pitchers with red veins, red flowers.

ssp. *alabemsis*:
Pitcher height: 25–48 cm (10–19 in).
Colours: yellow-green pitchers with red veins.

ssp. *gulfensis*:
43–57.5 cm (17–23 in) tall.
green pitchers and red veins.

ssp. *jonessi*:
51–68cm (20–27inches) in height.
Green pitchers with red veins. Bright red flowers.

ssp. *wherryi*:
Green in colour with red veins.

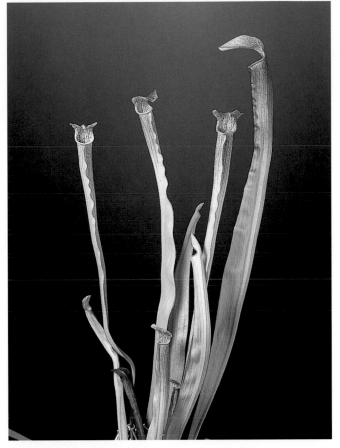

Above *Sarracenia rubra*

Below and over Pitcher plants have unusual nodding flowers.

Hybrids

Sarracenia species are easily cross-pollinated and there are a number of hybrids within this genus. Natural hybrids occur due to the proximity of some of the species in their native habitat. Additionally, many hybrids have been created in cultivation—there are literally hundreds.

Creating hybrids

You will need two separate species, preferably both in flower at the same time. Firstly, collect the pollen. When the pollen is ripe, it falls onto the umbrella-shaped style which is situated below the stamen. Fresh pollen can be collected from the inside surface of the style with a cotton bud.

With the cotton bud, brush the freshly collected pollen onto the stigma of the second plant. Continue this procedure daily until the flower dies and hopefully hybrid seeds will be created.

Propagation

Sarracenias can be propagated by either seeds, leaf cuttings or rhizome cutting.

SEEDS Sprinkle seeds onto moist sphagnum moss in a glass or plastic jar and cover with plastic. The humidity created will aid germination. Once seeds have germinated and are a few centimetres (1–2 inches) tall they are ready to plant into pots.

LEAF CUTTINGS When taking leaf cuttings, ensure that a small part of rhizome is attached. The cutting can then be placed in sphagnum moss in a container and sealed with plastic. Roots will eventually grow and the plant can be potted.

RHIZOME CUTTINGS The rhizome can be sectioned using a sharp knife. Depending on the size, the rhizome can be cut into two or three sections. Ensure that there are some roots attached to each section. This will ease re-growth. The sections can then be re-potted.

A hybrid, *S. courtii x swaniana*

Keeping and caring for your plant

If given the correct conditions, the *Sarracenia* can prove to be a hardy and attractive house plant.

POTTING MIX Three parts peat moss with one part sand.

LIGHT Full sunlight.

WATERING Plenty of water during summer through a water tray. Preferably, this should be rain water, or tap water allowed to sit for a few days. During winter the water supply should be reduced in order to allow dormancy. Remove plant from water tray and water only once a week. The pitchers will die off during this period. However, the rhizome will continue to grow. Many growers cut off all remaining pitchers to induce dormancy and reduce any risk of disease. When summer arrives, increase water and plant will produce new pitchers which will be bigger and stronger than the previous year.

Problem solving

The pitchers will grow but the tops dry out and turn brown.	The plant is receiving too much heat and the sun is burning the tops of the pitchers. You should move the plant to receive less sunlight. Often moving the plant to a lower position can often help i.e. if it is sitting on the top of a bench, you can drop it down to a lower level.
The pitcher stem is growing inconsistently with bends and appearing wiry.	It is not receiving enough water. During the growing stage, pitchers require an abundance of water.

6

Cobra lily

Family: Sarracianeae
Botanical name: *Darlingtonia california*
Distribution: California, Oregon, USA. See map.

The cobra lily obtains its name from the resemblance that an adult plant has with a cobra, about to strike its prey. With its cobra-like head and two threatening fangs, this species is certainly one of the more impressive and sought-after carnivorous plants.

Whilst closely related to the *Sarracenia*, the cobra lily is the only member of its genus. It can be found near the Pacific coast in Oregon and northern California in the USA, mainly on mountains. However, it has been seen growing near sea level.

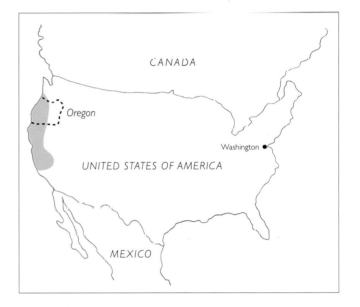

Capturing its prey

Insects are lured to the cobra lily through its small nectar glands which secrete sweet-tasting nectar. These glands are dispersed all over the front of the plant and are more numerous on the fang-like structure which is called the 'fishtail'. The insect tastes the nectar and slowly makes its way towards the mouth of the plant as the nectar is strongest near the mouth. Both the wing at the front and the fishtail lead the insect directly to the mouth.

On entering the mouth the insect is confused, and its ability to find the exit is made all the more difficult by the transparent windows which are abundant at the roof of the dome. The insect attempts to exit through these windows only to find that an exit is unavailable.

Within the ceiling of the plant are numerous short, backward-pointing hairs. These hairs encourage the insect to walk towards the back of the trap where it encounters a slippery smooth surface, loses its footing and falls to the bottom into the water. Escape is impossible, as the wings are quickly soaked and the long downward-pointing hairs directly above the surface of the water inhibit any chance of crawling out. The insect is slowly broken down and absorbed by the pitcher.

Opposite A mature cobra lily pitcher

Above and left The cobra lily obtains its name from the resemblance that a pitcher has with a cobra about to strike its prey.

Below A clump of cobra lily pitchers

Keeping and caring for your plant

As with all carnivorous plants, it is essential to understand the native growing conditions in order to grow plants at home. Being a mountain dweller, this species is watered through the cool mountainous rivers which flow in its native habitat. Therefore, the cobra lily requires its root system to be kept cool and moist at all times.

This plant prefers colder climates and it is extremely difficult to maintain a healthy species in hot conditions. It is consequently not recommended for these areas. Once temperatures exceed 30° Celsius (86° Fahrenheit) the plant will suffer and often die.

This species experiences a winter dormancy. During spring, a nodding reddish flower on a long steam appears from the centre of the cluster.

POTTING MIXTURE A peat/sand mix is appropriate, otherwise the cobra lily can be potted in pure sphagnum moss which will assist a cool root system. A clay or terracotta pot (or a polystyrene fruit box) will assist in maintaining cooler temperatures for the root system.

LIGHT Filtered light. Care must be taken to ensure plant doesn't overheat. A lack of direct sunlight does not seem to cause any deformities.

WATERING Water once or twice a day during the warmer months. During winter dormancy, only once a week will suffice.

Propagation

RHIZOME DIVISION The adult rhizome can be divided at the various growth points. The cutting can then be re-potted and roots will develop after about a month. Care must be taken not to disturb the new roots, as they can be easily broken and the plant will die. New pitchers should appear after approximately three months.

SEEDS Cobra lily seeds should be stratified to increase the chance of success. The stratification process simulates the natural cold winter to which the seeds are normally subjected before they sprout in summer. To stratify, the seeds are first placed in a sealed jar of moist sphagnum moss. It is then allowed to stay in a refrigerator for at least six weeks.

The seeds can then be removed and placed in a potting mixture. Maintain high humidity and moisture.

Juvenile leaves which are quite different in appearance to a mature pitcher, are produced first. During its second stage of growth, mature leaves begin to appear in a cluster. The new growth will first face the centre of the plant and then unusually twist around to face the outside.

Above The flower of the cobra lily

Below Once the flower is fertilised, it moves to an upright form.

7

Sun pitcher

Family: Sarraceniaceae
Botanical name: *Heliamphora*
Distribution: Venezuela. See map.

There are six known species of sun pitchers which survive in an environment of constant high humidity and near continuous rainfall with average rainfalls often exceeding 254 cm (100 in). All six species can be found on the top of the mountain plateaus of the Guiana highlands which are in Venezuela, South America. These flat-topped, often featureless mountains extend over a vast area and reach altitudes of between 1000 and 3000 m (3200–9800 ft) above sea level before suddenly reaching an abrupt end at a steep cliff face.

Mount Auyin-Tepui extends over more than 700 sq km (270 sq m) and is home to Angel Falls, which plunges 979 m (3212 ft) down the wall of the mountain and is the longest waterfall in the world. The area has been described as one of the wettest places on earth with the air so moist that there is a continuous spray of misting rain in the atmosphere. Even though these plants are in close proximity to the equator they experience cool nights due to the high altitudes in which they survive.

The sun pitcher has been suggested as the possible missing link between carnivorous and non-carnivorous plants due to the isolation of the mountains and primitive structure of the plant. Some of the rock in the area has been dated at more than a billion years old.

This genus is from the Sarraceniaceae family and captures its prey in a similar manner to all pitcher plants. It is one of the most primitive carnivorous plants in appearance and is basically a leaf which has joined at its margins to form a tube.

The inside of the tube consists of nectar glands which attract the insect and long downward-pointing hairs which cause the prey to slip and fall into the digestive juices in the bottom of the tube.

Opposite *Heliamphora heterodoxa*

Above *Heliamphora minor*

Each species features an unusual little spoon on top of the pitcher. This little growth called the bell produces an abundance of nectar and lures insects to the top of the tube. Once the insect is above the pitcher and suckling on the nectar, one little slip and it will fall to its watery grave. The insect soon drowns and is absorbed as nutrition for the plant.

Heliamphora heterodoxa

Distribution: Mount Ptari-Tepui, Venezuela
Variations: *heterodoxa*
          exappendiculata
          glabra

The pitchers range in height from 15–25 cm (6–10in) with a thin red line on the rim. Flowers are pink and white.

Heliamphora ionasi

Distribution: Ilu-Tepui, Venezuela
The pitchers of this species are the largest in this genus growing up to 46 cm (18 in) in height. The wide flared pitchers become red with age and possess a large spoon.

Heliamphora minor

Distribution: Mount Auyan-Tepui, Venezuela
This is the smallest in the genus which grows up to 7.5 cm (3 in) in height. The pitchers develop in colour from green to burgundy depending on the quantity of sunlight.

Heliamphora neblinae

Distribution: Cerro de la Neblina, Venezuela
Variations: *neblinae*—white flowers
          parva—pink flowers
          viridis—green flowers

Yellowish-green pitchers which grow up to 25 cm (10 in) in height.

Heliamphora nutans

Distribution: Mount Roraima, Venezuela
Pitchers grow up to 15 cm (6 in long).

Heliamphora tatei

Distribution: Mount Duida, Venezuela
Variations: *tatei*
          macdonaldae—lacking hairs
          neblinae

This species is unique in that it produces shrubby stems which grow up to 4 m (13 ft) tall.

Keeping and caring for your plant

This genus is difficult to obtain and relatively new to growers. It is not a recommended plant for new growers.

The *Heliamphora* grows through a rhizome (underground stem) and prefers a relatively stable environment with constant high humidity and day temperatures in the range of 16° to 27° Celsius (61° to 81° Fahrenheit) and night temperatures of between 5° to 15° Celsius (41° to 59° Fahrenheit). Once temperatures exceed 30° Celsius (86° Fahrenheit) for a sustained period the plants have a tendency to dry out and the leaves burn.

The best success with this genus has been achieved through growing in an environment suitable for tropical pitcher plants.

POTTING MIX The most successful potting mix is live sphagnum moss with perlite. A deep 15 cm (6 in) pot is recommended.

WATERING It is best to water through a mist system from above a few times a day. This achieves the required humidity and a desired cooling effect on the leaves in the warmer temperatures. If the temperature exceeds 30° Celsius (86° Fahrenheit) watering should be increased.

LIGHT Direct sunlight should be avoided due to ease of burning pitchers. Filtered light is best.

GROWING TIPS Whilst sun pitchers are rhizome growing plants, they detest a disturbance to the root system. Splitting the rhizome as with other genera is not recommended for this genus. It is advised to allow them to continue to grow and thrive, repotting them to larger pots when they have outgrown their current environment.

When old pitchers have become dry, it is best to remove them by cutting them off with a pair of fine pointed scissors, allowing room for new pitchers to grow.

Propagation

SEED Reproduction from seed is slow with germination taking up to three months. Sow in a peat/sand mix and keep damp in low light.

RHIZOME DIVISION Whilst it is possible to divide the plant, it is not recommended due to risk of losing the entire species.

Above *Heliamphora heterodoxa*

Below *Heliamphora nutans*

8

Albany pitcher plant

Family: Cephalotaceae
Botanical name: *Cephalotus follicularis*
Distribution: south-west of Western Australia. See map.

An enigma in the carnivorous plant world, this pitcher plant grows exclusively in the peaty swamps amongst dense scrub and reeds along the south coast of Western Australia. The West Australian or Albany pitcher plant is the only plant in its genus and its family. It is increasingly difficult to locate in its natural habitat due to pressures of farmland with cattle trampling on the plants.

It grows through a very thick branching rhizome which spreads underground in the wild and maintains the moisture that the plant requires. *Cephalotus* produces pitchers that generally grow up to 5 cm (2 in) in size and form in a round cluster. The colour of the pitcher varies from green to dark burgundy, depending on the quantity of sunlight it receives. Alongside the pitchers, the plant also grows non-carnivorous leaves during summer.

During summer, a flower scape, which grows up to 60 cm (24 in) appears bearing small white flowers with no petals open.

Trapping insects

Similar to other pitcher plants, the *Cephalotus* is a passive trap and relies on insects to crawl inside the pitcher. When the pitcher reaches full size, its lid opens, allowing it to feed on prey. The lid remains open for the life of the pitcher.

The West Australian pitcher plant features three ridges on the outside of the pitcher which act as a path for insects to crawl up, towards the nectar. This nectar is situated at the entrance to entice insects, which in turn lose their footing and fall into its digestive fluids. The ribbed and spined rim make it virtually impossible for insects to escape.

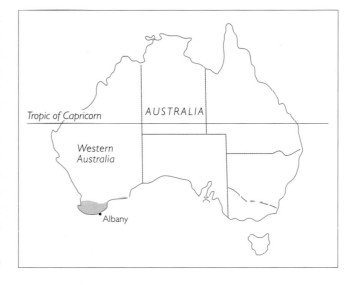

Opposite Albany pitcher plant—close-up of pitcher

Keeping and caring for your plant

The most common cause of failure with this species is rootrot where the soil is kept too wet.

POTTING MIX　The *Cephalotus* requires a relatively open mix to prevent a build up of an excess of water. The recommended mixture is 50% peat moss, 25% sand and 25% vermiculite. Sphagnum moss can be placed on the surface to maintain a high humidity level.

WATERING　If it is potted in an adequately large pot, (about a 15 cm full length pot is suitable) it can be placed within a tray of water in the warmer months. However, watering from above is probably best. During winter, the soil should only be kept damp and therefore must be removed from the tray of water as it can be susceptible to rootrot.

LIGHT　Full sun will produce a beautiful burgundy colour on the pitchers. However, care must be taken when the temperatures exceed 35° Celsius (95° Fahrenheit) as the plant can easily burn. Filtered light all year round is quite acceptable.

Propagation

RHIZOME CUTTINGS　The most successful method of reproduction is to take cuttings from the rhizome growing underground. This is achieved through removing the plant from the pot and cutting a healthy rhizome into sections of about 5 cm (2 in). They should then be dipped in a rooting hormone, sprayed with a fungicide and placed under the soil.

A new plant should appear in about a month.

LEAF CUTTINGS　Reproduction is also possible through obtaining leaf or pitcher cuttings. Remove the cutting close to the rhizome, spray with fungicide and place it within a potting mixture. It should develop roots and re-grow within a month.

SEEDS　It is possible to cultivate through seed. However, seed is difficult to obtain and seedlings are very slow to grow. They should be placed in a potting mixture and maintained with constant warmth, damp and humidity. Germination may take many months.

The green colouring of the Albany pitcher plant shown at right indicates that it has been grown in the shade or in lower light levels.

The plant illustrated below shows the burgundy colouring of a plant grown in full sunlight.

9

Tropical pitcher plant

Family: Nepenthaceae
Botanical name: *Nepenthes*
Distribution: South-East Asia, Australia, Madagascar, India.

The eighty-two species of *Nepenthes* are amongst the most sought-after and spectacular of all carnivorous plants. They grow mainly in the exotic tropical rainforest regions of South-East Asia. They are prolific in Borneo and Sumatra.

Folklore abounds about this genus, including references to traditional uses of it as a rice cooker, medicine and a source of water. An early explorer into Borneo in 1880, Frederick Burbidge, wrote:

The next difficulty was to obtain water, since the men we had sent for it returned empty-handed. In wandering in search of more. I came upon a patch of the large *Nepenthes*, from the old pitchers of which I was able to augment my supply by carefully pouring off the rainwater from a rather liberal understratum of flies, ants and other insect debris.

Right *Nepenthes ventricosa*

Opposite *Nepenthes alata*, highland species

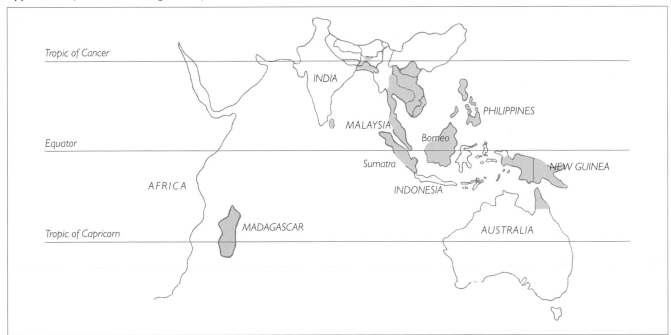

Tropic of Cancer

INDIA

PHILIPPINES

MALAYSIA

Borneo

Equator

Sumatra

NEW GUINEA

AFRICA

INDONESIA

Tropic of Capricorn

MADAGASCAR

AUSTRALIA

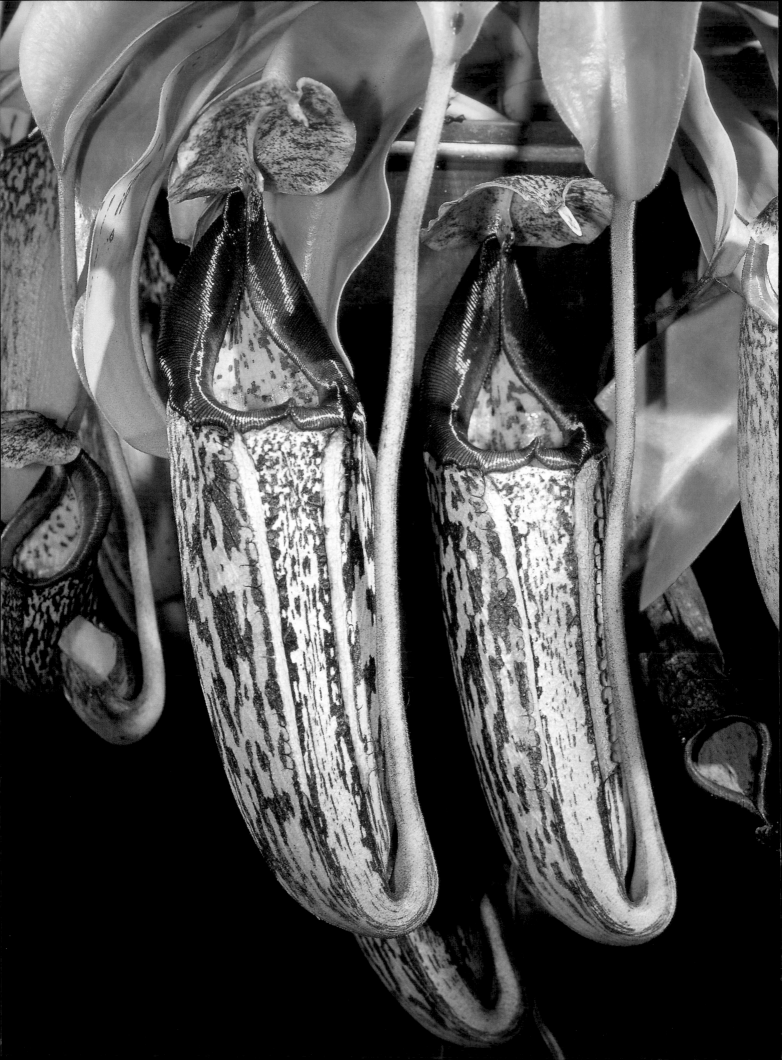

He also recorded in 1897, 'when I was staying with the headman of the Kadyans on the Lawas river, his people gave me delicious rice cooked in the pitchers, as a sweetmeat to be eaten with jungle fruit or bananas'.

The general appearance of a *Nepenthes* includes a thick vertical stem in the centre with large non-carnivorous leaves protruding and growing up to 50 cm (20 in) in length. At the tip of the leaf is a tendril which is often used for the plant to twist itself onto a tree.

Some of the species are vigorous climbers and can grow up to 15 m (50 ft) in height.

At the tip of the tendril a most amazing growth occurs. What starts as a tiny deformity, soon enlarges and then inflates into one of nature's wonders. Each species produces its own colourful and distinctively shaped pitcher. *Nepenthes rajah*, the king of them all, produces pitchers the size of footballs and has been known to capture rats.

To those who are considering growing this genus, it must be stressed that they are tropical plants and require specialised growing conditions and dedication if attempted in temperate climates.

Types

There are two types of *Nepenthes*:

Lowland species. A group which grows within the rainforest jungle in very hot and humid conditions at temperatures of between 16° Celsius (61° Fahrenheit) and 32° Celsius (90° Fahrenheit) with humidity levels constantly above 70%.

Highland species. This group grows above the jungle canopies at altitudes greater than 1000 m (0.6 mile). The higher altitude species survive in lower temperatures with night temperatures sometimes dropping to freezing. This is the group recommended to grow in a temperate climate.

Above *Nepenthes alata* has twined itself onto a branch.

Opposite *Nepenthes maxima*

Below Hybrid pitcher plant, *Nepenthes maxima × veitchii*

Below right *Nepenthes rajah* can hold up to two litres of water.

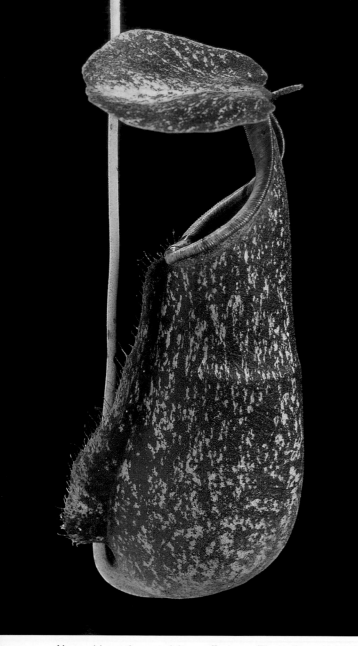

Above *Nepenthes mirabilis* × *rafflesiana* (Photo: Terry Knight)

Below Growing stages of pitcher

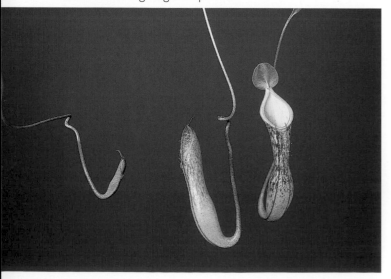

Pitchers

Each species produces two distinct types of pitchers:

Lower pitcher. The lower pitcher is produced during the first few years of growth. The tendril is usually attached to the front of the pitcher. Lower pitchers are generally more colourful and often larger than the upper pitcher.

Upper pitcher. Once a plant has grown to a significant height, upper pitchers are produced. The tendril is attached to the rear of the pitcher through a loop which forms. This tendril loop is used to attach itself to a nearby tree, enabling it to climb. The upper pitcher can sometimes be remarkably different to the lower pitchers.

The pitcher

Each species of *Nepenthes* has a pitcher with distinctively different size, colour and shape. This means they are a rewarding species for the avid carnivorous plant collector.

THE LID   Each species consists of a lid which is static for the life of the pitcher. Its function is to produce nectar and therefore enable it to lure and capture prey. Another purpose it serves is to act as an umbrella to protect the pitcher from the heavy tropical rain storms.

THE RIM   Many species produce a brightly red-coloured rim on the edge of the pitcher. This is often ribbed and is a beautiful feature of some species. The rim's function is to produce nectar and attract insects through its often bright colour.

THE SPUR   A spur appears on some species. *Nepenthes* is often raided by lizards and birds that eat insects which have fallen into the pitcher. It is believed that the spur has evolved as a thorny deterrent to these scavengers.

FRONTAL WING AND RIB   The frontal wing and rib assist the species to capture prey. The wings run parallel at the front of the pitcher towards the rim and act as a path, enticing them to travel upwards and into the trap.

Capturing insects

Similar to the *Sarracenia*, the *Nepenthes* is a passive carnivore and needs to entice its prey to enter the pitcher. This is achieved through the secretion of sweet-tasting nectar that seduces insects to enter the pitcher and abounds below the lid and on the rim.

When an insect enters the area, it often strays further into the pitcher. Once the prey is inside, the waxy sides offer little support. It slips downwards and falls into the deadly cocktail of digestive fluids.

The victim soon drowns and is absorbed as food for the plant.

Keeping and caring for your plant

Whilst *Nepenthes* is an extremely rewarding genus to cultivate, it requires constant warmth and humidity which is difficult to maintain all year-round.

Most growers living in temperate climates maintain suitable conditions through building a hothouse. The hothouse generally includes a sprinkler system on a timer to maintain humidity and a heating system to keep warmth during winter. Highland species are recommended for this environment, due to their tolerance of cooler temperatures.

However, if they are located in the tropics, the lowland species flourish outdoors with minimal care. The only requirement is regular daily watering and filtered light. I would recommend monitoring humidity levels with a hygrometer to ensure at least 70% humidity at all times. An overhead spray system and its subsequent evaporation maintains a high humidity.

POTTING MIXTURE An effective all-purpose potting mixture is commercially available orchid mix. Otherwise, you can use pine bark mixed with peat moss and coarse river sand. The essential requirement is an open mix which drains freely and quickly.

GROWING TIP Damp sphagnum moss placed on top of the potting mixture is recommended. The moisture produced assists in maintaining a higher humidity level for the plant.

LIGHT Filtered light. Whilst *Nepenthes* enjoy sunlight, which increases the beauty, colour and size of pitchers, caution must be observed to avoid burning the leaves and pitchers. Each species requires different quantities of sunlight. A general recommendation is to allow a few hours of early morning sunlight each day.

HUMIDITY Ideally, at least 70% humidity is recommended at all times

WATERING The *Nepenthes* must not be kept in a bowl of water due to the risk of rootrot. Daily overhead watering through a mist system is recommended. However, a watering can to simulate the regular rainfall of a tropical rainforest is acceptable.

Tap water is generally satisfactory.

TEMPERATURE REQUIREMENTS

Lowland species   15°–30° C (59°–86° F)
Highland species   10°–30° C (50°–86° F)

FERTILISER Unlike most other genera of carnivorous plants, *Nepenthes* thrive on the regular addition of fertiliser. A liquid fertiliser that is high in nitrogen is recommended. An example is a fertiliser used for epiphytes or orchids.

A fortnightly dose of a half-strength mixture during the growing season will increase growth drastically.

Above Nepenthes bicalcalarta grows its distinctive twin fangs.

Below Nepenthes lowii

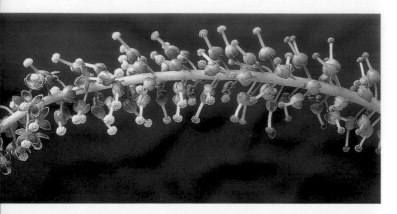

Flowering

Nepenthes flower annually, usually in spring. The flowers are small and not a prominent feature of the genus. The plants are unisexual (producing exclusively male or female flowers) and therefore in order to pollinate a species, both a male and female plant are required. It is virtually impossible to distinguish between male and female plants before flowering and the grower must wait until the plant flowers to discover the sex of the species.

Left *Nepenthes* flowers: male, upper picture; female, lower picture

Below left *Nepenthes ventricosa*

Below *Nepenthes bicalcalarta*, lowland species

Propagation

SEEDS Successful propagation through seed depends on obtaining fresh seed; usually it should be no more than one month old. However, due to the unisexual nature of a *Nepenthes*, fresh seed is relatively difficult to obtain. Seed should be sown in an open drained mix such as a peat/sand mix or a fine orchid mix. The pot should be placed in a heating tray to ensure warmth and humidity levels are kept constantly high. Depending on their freshness, seeds can take up to twelve weeks to sprout.

CUTTINGS The simplest method of propagation is from cuttings of a mature plant.

(i) A 45° cut should be made on the stem between two leaves.

(ii) The leaves can then be trimmed back about half way up the leaf. This method enables the stem to continue photosynthesis whilst allowing the plant to direct all its growing energy into new leaves.

(iii) The stem is dipped in a rooting hormone which seals the base of the stem.

(iv) The cutting can now be placed in a suitable potting mix, such as used for seeds. New growth should appear within a month.

Hybrids

Numerous hybrids are available. Some occur naturally but most are developed in cultivation. They can be produced through the cross-fertilisation of male and female flowers from different species.

A phenomenon known as hybrid vigour ensures hybrids are much hardier than a pure species. Therefore, it is recommended that new growers begin with hybrids as success is much more likely.

Nepenthes maxima, upper pitcher

Problem solving

The foliage is growing well but it is not producing pitchers or is producing very small pitchers.	This is an indication that you are not simulating the correct environment for the plant to thrive. It usually means that humidity levels and/or light levels are too low.
The leaves seem to be drying out and the plant is dying.	Humidity and light are much too low.
The leaves seem to be showing signs of burning.	This indicates too much sun. Alternatively the same symptom could occur if the plant is subjected to temperatures below the recommended levels.

10

Butterwort

Family: Lentibulariaceae
Botanical name: *Pinguicula* (Latin for 'the little greasy')
Distribution: See map.

The butterwort derives its name from the greasy surface of its leaves. The buttery feel occurs due to the numerous tiny glands on the leaf surface. On touching the leaves, insects are instantly glued and captured in a similar fashion to the sundew.

There are about 75 species found mainly in North and South America, and Europe. Mexico is the predominant location for butterworts with about 40 species native to the country. During the past decade, many new species have been discovered in Mexico due mainly to numerous field trips through the country by Dr Lau, a missionary. An unusual aspect of the genus is that some species grow two totally different leaves in summer and winter. The winter leaves are usually non-carnivorous.

The most attractive feature of this genus is its beautiful small flowers, with some species flowering regularly throughout the year.

Above A new butterwort species from Mexico

Opposite An attractive feature of the butterwort is its flowers.

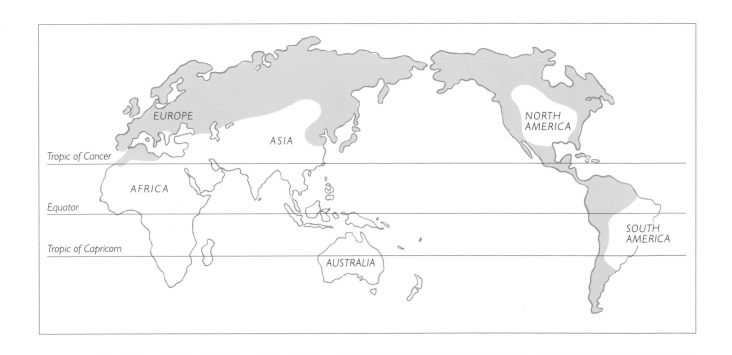

Above *Pinguicula moranensis* hybrid

Below Another new species from Mexico

Left Winter rosette of *Pinguicula moranensis*

The growing environment

Anyone intending to grow butterworts must appreciate the different conditions required by (a) temperate and (b) tropical species.

Temperate or cool-growing species

Found mainly in the cooler climates of Europe, these species adapt to the sometimes freezing temperatures by entering a dormancy period by producing a hibernacula (bud) during the winter.

During this period they produce gemmae (a gemma is an asexual body which detaches itself from the parent to reproduce itself). Gemmae can easily be flicked from the plant to produce a new sprout. In their native habitat the winter rains wash the gemmae from the plant to another location and increase their population.

Tropical/sub-tropical or warm-growing species

Found mainly in Mexico, South America, southern Europe and southern United States these species grow in warmer climates and due to their milder environment do not need any dormancy period.

The different forms

Both the temperate and tropical species have two distinct forms:

The one-leaved or homophyllous species. These species produce the same leaves all year round and will generally flower more than once during the year.

The two-leaved or heterophyllous species. Some species have the unusual habit of producing two distinctly different leaf forms throughout the year. They are generally called summer and winter leaves. The winter leaves form in a tight bud and can often be non-carnivorous.

Growing butterworts
The temperate species

This should be the preferred group to grow in the cooler climates.

POTTING MIX Most butterworts produce a very short root system and can be grown in short pots with a three part peat moss to one part sand mix. Otherwise some species prefer the straight sphagnum moss mix in the top half of the pot with the peat/sand mix in the bottom half of the pot to maintain the moisture.

LIGHT Filtered light.

Tropical species

POTTING MIX Depending on the species, pure sphagnum moss, straight vermiculite or perlite and the standard three parts peat moss to one part sand or vermiculite have all been used successfully.

The favourable mix for the Mexican species is pure live sphagnum moss.

LIGHT Filtered light.

humidity High humidity, at least 40% at all times.

WATERING For the Mexican species, water from above and avoid wetting leaves as they can be prone to rootrot. Most other species can be placed in 2 cm (1 in) of water during summer and removed from the tray and lightly watered during winter.

TEMPERATURE Temperatures should be maintained between 10° and 30° degrees Celsius (50°–86° Fahrenheit).

Propagation

Butterworts are relatively easy to propagate. The simplest method is to obtain leaf cuttings when the new summer leaves have formed. They can then be placed into the potting mix and a new plant will be produced in about a month.

If fresh seed is available, it can be germinated by sprinkling onto a moist potting mix and allowed to sit in a light and humid environment.

Another new species from Me...

Pinguicula pri...

11

Bladderwort

Family: Lentibulariaceae
Botanical name: *Utricularia* (Latin for 'bagpipe')
Distribution: See map.

The bladderwort was first classified in 1753 by Carl Linnaeus. It receives its name from the trapping mechanism, a tiny, but very efficient bladder that is able to capture mosquito larvae, small tadpoles and any other tiny creature.

It was ranked a very close second by Charles Darwin as the 'most wonderful plant in the world'. He was amazed by the ingenious trap which not only lured prey, but also sucked them into the deadly chamber.

It is the most abundant genus of carnivorous plants with over 215 species, found mainly in the warmer climates of South America, Australia, Africa and Asia.

Many species are totally devoid of any leaves and can only be easily distinguished from one another through the often beautiful flower which appears on the stem.

A very unusual property of this genus is that it survives without any root system throughout its entire life. Underneath the soil surface or beneath the water, the bladderwort forms branches which produce bladders that capture tiny insects and provide its nutritional source.

Above A typical bladderwort with traps underneath the surface

Opposite *Utricularia leptoplectra* in its native habitat (Photo: Terry Knight)

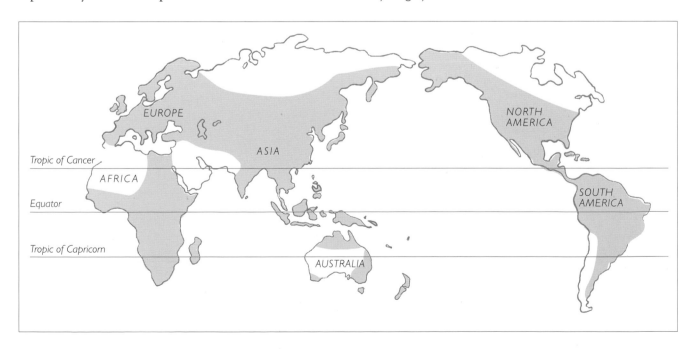

Bladder awaits its prey.

A mosquito strays near awaiting trap.

Mosquito touches sensitive trigger hairs.

On touching the hairs, the mosquito is sucked into the trap.

The bladder will ingest the mosquito as its food.

Above A mosuito larvae has strayed near an awaiting trap. It is quickly sucked into the bladder as food for the plant.

Below *Utricularia bisquamata*

The trap

The bladderwort consists of many tiny traps, usually smaller than a pinhead, which grow either underground or underwater on the end of shoots. The trap is transparent and varies in shape. Depending on the species, it can be round, oval or more cylindrical.

The bladder is a complex structure consisting of trigger hairs at the entrance. The hairs are protected by larger stalks which prevent larger insects from falsely triggering the trap.

As tiny insects stray beside the bladder, they touch the trigger hairs which instantly open the trap inwardly. This inward force creates a vacuum which pulls water and insect into the bladder and closes immediately in fractions of a second.

Once trapped, enzymes and acids are released and slowly digest the victim.

Bladderworts survive in a variety of habitats:
They can be either:
- aquatic (living in water and floating)
- rheophytes (living in water but attached to ground)
- terrestrial (living on land)
- epiphytic (living on trees)
- lithophytes (living on rocks)
- 60% are terrestrial.

Above *Utricularia fulva* growing on rocks (Photo: Terry Knight)

Below The traps appear in a variety of bizarre shapes.

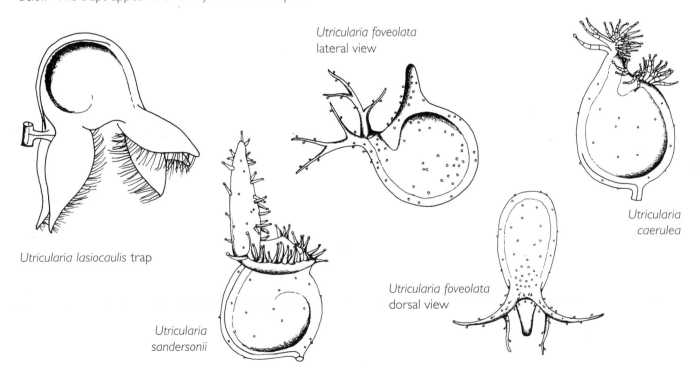

Utricularia foveolata
lateral view

Utricularia lasiocaulis trap

Utricularia sandersonii

Utricularia foveolata
dorsal view

Utricularia caerulea

Keeping and caring for your plant

Due to the abundance of different species, it is difficult to provide accurate growing information on the entire group. The following information exists as a guide to the different types of growing environments for bladderworts.

As with any plant, it is best to choose species which survive in climates similar to your own. The listing at the back of the book should be used as a guide.

Aquatic species

A water tank is required for aquatic species. A layer of peat moss should be added to the bottom of the tank. It can then be filled with water, preferably rain water. The water will be cloudy for the first few days until the peat moss settles. It is advisable to wait for the water to settle before adding plants. The tank can be placed in an area of filtered light.

These plants require varying degrees of acidity in the water, therefore some experimentation and regular pH checks are needed. A pH gauge can be purchased from your nearest aquarium.

I have observed that, if the pH is incorrect, whilst the plant will survive, bladders will not grow.

The most dangerous enemy to the aquatic varieties is algae, the onset of which can easily kill all your plants. Microscopic algae is noticeable as a cloudy formation on the water surface. I have had success with treating algae through purchasing commercially available formulas obtainable from an aquarium. Follow the instructions carefully and results should be obtained within a week.

Propagation

The simplest method of propagation is to take stem cuttings. Most aquatic species will multiply like weeds if maintained in the correct environment.

Left *Utricularia dichotoma*

Terrestrial and rheophytic species

Many of this group survive in extremely wet areas bordering watercourses, such as swamps, lagoons, etc. In cultivating, generally a mix of two parts peat moss with one part coarse river sand is appropriate. Some species will survive, grown in straight live sphagnum moss. The pot must be kept in a tray of water and placed in a filtered sunlight position.

Propagation

LEAF CUTTINGS The species which grow leaves can be propagated through leaf cuttings. Simply cut the leaf off just above the soil level and place it on a bed of sphagnum moss. Lightly cover the cutting with small pieces of moss. Place the container in a warm and humid environment, such as a terrarium. Otherwise enclose it with a plastic bottle container cut in half. After approximately a month, roots and new leaves will form. The plant is now ready to pot

SEED As a general rule, fresh seed can be sown in a peat/sand mix and placed in a humid, filtered light position within a tray of water.

Epiphytic species

Growing in the South American rainforests, this group is found surviving on the trunks and branches of trees.

They are recommended for warmer climates. The most suitable potting mix is orchid bark mixed with sphagnum moss. Being rainforest plants, they prefer warmth, humidity and low light. They can be watered by tray or an overhead spray system which will assist in maintaining a high humidity.

Above *Utricularia leptoplectra* flower (Photo: Terry Knight)

12

Carnivorous home garden

Carnivorous plants can make a fascinating addition to your garden. Following arc some suggested ideas and tips to producing your own carnivorous home garden.

Outdoor gardening
The bog garden
The bog garden simulates the wet swampy conditions in which many carnivorous plants survive.

(i) Selecting the area
The area chosen should ideally receive full sunlight in the morning followed by filtered light in the afternoon. Therefore it should be protected by trees ensuring that your plants will not burn in the hot afternoon summer sun.

(ii) Creating the bog garden
There are many options in creating a bog garden.

Dig a hole about 60 cm (2 ft) deep. The length and width are totally up to the individual. The hole should be lined with thick plastic to ensure the area can remain moist. A thin layer of coarse river sand can then be placed on top of the plastic. Other suggestions include using an old bathtub or commercially available ponds which are obtainable at the nursery.

The next step is to install the watering system. I have found the most effective watering system is a reticulation system inside the hole. The pipe is laid on top of the sand with four to six outlets, depending on the size of the hole. The pipe can then have a hose connection nearby. This system ensures that water will soak thoroughly within the bog garden

The hole is now ready to fill with a peat/sand mixture.

Above right A small garden greenhouse can provide the ideal environment for tropical carnivorous plants.

Right A raised bog garden in a shadehouse

Opposite Carnivorous plants such as pitcher plants are ideal for growing in containers.

(iii) Selection of plants

The type of plants chosen for your garden should be those that are suitable for your climatic conditions. Once you understand the native growing environment of different varieties, selection will become easy.

In temperate zones, most pitcher plants and Venus fly traps can grow well outdoors. There should be a selection of sundews and bladderworts suitable for your climate. Tall plants should be in the back with smaller plants towards the front for best aesthetic effect.

In tropical and hot environments, there are limitations to which plants can grow outdoors in the sunlight. In such localities, you may be limited to tropical sundews and some terrestrial bladderworts which tolerate the hot sun.

Most plants will experience stress and die back once planted in a new environment. However, most will recover and grow back stronger than ever.

Carnivorous pond

An interesting addition to your garden could include a carnivorous pond. Commercially manufactured ponds are obtainable from your local nursery. The pond can then be dug into your garden, filled with water and an array of bladderworts placed within it.

It is advisable to choose the species which survives in your climate and remember that aquatic bladderworts prefer acidic water.

Waterlilies and reeds (if available) could also be added to simulate the natural conditions of a pond.

Tropical rainforest

Simulating a tropical rainforest in your garden can make an interesting area for any tropical climate.
Necessary requirements:
• tropical weather
• large trees for canopies
• shade cloth to prevent bright sunlight
• spray system for watering

Long-term planning is required to correctly simulate the conditions of a tropical rainforest. The resulting area can be an excellent environment for Nepenthes and a fascinating habitat which will enthrall your visitors.

Above left Carnivorous plants growing in a bog garden

Left Pitcher plants growing in a greenhouse

Indoor gardening
Terrariums

If space outdoors is limited, an ideal alternative to keeping plants is in the form of a terrarium, which is basically a sealed glass or plastic container which forms its own unique environment.

As the atmosphere within a terrarium is ideal for any plant, the shape of the enclosure must reflect the type of plant that you are attempting to grow inside, i.e. *Sarracenia* require taller enclosures whereas Venus fly traps, sundews, *Nepenthes* etc. need a much wider area.

A general peat/sand mix is appropriate with a covering of sphagnum moss. When the plants have been added, fill with enough water to ensure the soil is damp. Once this is done the container can be sealed and watering is no longer required for a substantial period.

When the plants are first placed within the enclosure, they will experience climatisation and can initially die back. However, they should re-grow healthily in the environment.

The terrarium should be placed in a light area away from direct sunlight preventing overheating within the enclosure. As this is an ideal growing environment, care must be taken to prevent fungus from growing. Therefore, regular spraying of fungicide is necessary.

A potting suggestion with a self-watering pot

An inexpensive aquarium with a lid can be used as an ideal terrarium.

13

Pests and diseases

Like most other plant species, carnivorous plants have their enemies.

Whilst it is virtually impossible to prevent any pests and diseases from attacking your precious collection, the best advice available is for early detection and prompt treatment which will prevent any subsequent serious damage or spreading to other plants.

Following is a list of the common pests and diseases which affect carnivorous plants. I have not quoted specific products deliberately due to the variety of products available in different countries. It is important to first diagnose the problem and then consult your local nursery to locate a suitable product which is available.

The diseases

These are problems which are caused by living microscopic organisms. Fungi, and algae are the most common culprits in this category.

Fungi

There are over 15 000 species which are either parasites (living on live tissue) or saprophytes (living on dead tissue). Mildew is a commonly known form of fungus. These organisms generally suck the nutrition from the plant tissue to survive. Fungus is seen more often on plants which are in conditions of low light and warm weather.

SYMPTOMS The plant generally develops white blotches which will rapidly increase in size. The plant could then turn grey or black as the chlorophyll is sucked out of it.

TREATMENT The affected pitchers or leaves should be cut off and either burnt or separated out from other plants. The area should then be sprayed with a suitable fungicide.

Rootrot

Rootrot is a common and very deadly problem attacking many carnivorous plants if they are kept in the wrong conditions. Due to the need for some species to be kept wet during summer, it is important to ensure the plants do not become too wet during winter. Remember that most of these species need much less watering in the winter due to the cooler weather. Leaving your plants too wet could cause rootrot that attacks the plant through its root system or rhizome, causing it to wilt underground.

SYMPTOMS This is a difficult problem to detect early due to its attacking the plant underground first. The most obvious symptom is a severe stunting in the growth of the plant. It will quickly spread to the stem and cause discoloration in the leaves.

TREATMENT Unfortunately, once rootrot is established in a plant, it is virtually impossible to overcome. The only possibility is to change the potting mix, spray with fungicide and reduce the watering. If the rootrot is rife in a tropical pitcher plant, the best suggestion is to take a cutting from it.

Algae

Microscopic algae is a plant or plantlike substance which grows in water. There are many different forms. Algae only affects species of carnivorous plants which are aquatic, such as some bladderworts and the waterwheel plant. The onset of algae in a pool of water can spread rapidly and kill the plant species surviving in that environment.

SYMPTOM Microscopic algae can be detected generally as a thin cloudy film on the surface of the water.

TREATMENT Quite effective commercial products are available at aquariums.

Opposite Pitcher plants growing in the protection of a shadehouse

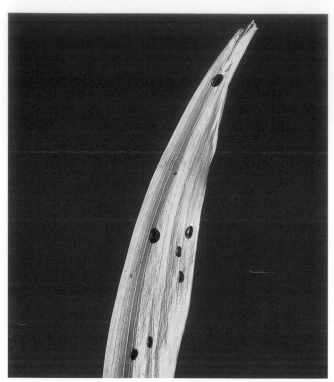

Scale growing on the leaf of a pitcher plant

The pests

Any animal can be a pest, with the most common being the insect.

Scale

Scale are shield–like insects which attach themselves onto leaves and stems. They feed by sucking the sap from the plant, and eventually weakening it. There are many different types, varying in colour from white, grey, brown mahogany or red. The scale forms small shells which appear on the leaf and are filled with eggs.
TREATMENT   Remove any badly affected leaves and treat with appropriate insecticide.

Mealy bugs

The individual mealy bug is tiny; however numbers of them usually live in colonies and appear as a white waxy powder on the plant. Some ants actually harvest them to use as a glue to build their nest.
TREATMENT   A suitable insecticide can be sprayed on the plant. Otherwise remove the bugs by cutting the affected leaves.

Aphids

Aphids are small, soft–bodied insects which can actually be seen by the naked eye. There are many species which can be green, yellow, bronze, brown grey, pink and black. They feed on plants by sucking the sap. The body is generally oval-shaped with two hollow stalks at the rear of the abdomen which excrete a sugary substance to feed their young.
TREATMENT   Use appropriate insecticide available.

The larger insects

Caterpillars, grasshoppers, snails and slugs are easily detected and should be simply removed by hand. Left unchecked, any of these insects could cause devastation by eating the plants almost entirely.

Glossary of terms

aquatic   Living in water.

cultivation   The act of cultivating. Growing plants in your own environment.

dormancy   The state of being inactive or asleep.

enzymes   Complex proteins that are produced by living cells.

epiphyte   (adjective EPIPHYTIC): A plant which grows on another plant but is not parasitic. It uses its host plant purely as support.

gemma   (plural GEMMAE): An asexual reproductive body that becomes detached from a parent plant

genus   (plural GENERA): A category to rank between the family and the species. e.g: the genus *Nepenthes*, the species *rajah*. Designated *N. rajah*.

lithophye   A plant that grows on rock.

peat moss   A moisture-retaining soil substance which has been gradually formed through the breakdown of other substances. It is usually acidic in nature.

perlite   A volcanic glass that has a concentric shelly structure that when expanded by heat forms a lightweight medium used to aerate soils.

propagation   The method of reproducing plants.

rheophyte   Living in water but attached to the ground.

rhizome   An underground horizontal plant stem.

rosette   A cluster of leaves in crowded circles or spirals arising basally from a crown.

scape   A flower stalk.

sphagnum moss   A natural organic material with high moisture-retention properties.

tissue culture   A chemical method of reproduction in which fragments of tissue are transferred to an artificial environment to enable them to reproduce. Using this method, up to one million plantlets can be produced in a year.

vermiculite   Any of various minerals which when treated with high temperatures give a lightweight, highly water-absorbent material to assist in aerating soils.

Appendix A

Carnivorous plant societies

Australia
Australian Carnivorous Plant Society Inc.
P.O. Box 391
St.Agnes
South Australia 5097

Carnivorous Plant Society of New South Wales
P.O. Box 87
Burwood
New South Wales 2134

Victorian Carnivorous Plant Society Inc.
P.O. Box 201
South Yarra
Victoria 3141

Belgium
Drosera V.Z.W.
Jasmijnstraat 34
B-9000 Gent

Canada
Pacific North West Carnivorous Plant Club
P.O. Box 42008
South Oak
Vancouver BC V5N 4J6

Czech Republic
Darwiniana
Ustavni 139
Praha 8 181 00

England
The Carnivorous Plant Society
3 Greys Road
GB Woodthorpe
Nottingham NGS 4GU

International Pinguicula Study Group
14 Rope Walk
Somerton
Somerset TA 12 6HZ

France
Association Dine's
15 Rue Des Pyrenes
Nay - Bourdettes
F-64800 Baudreix

Germany
Gesellschaft Fur Fleischfressende Pflanzen
Im Deutschprachigen Raum (GFP)
Zweibruckeentr, 31
D40625 Dusseldorf

Israel
Carnivorous Plant Society of Israel
Newe-Ya'ar Research Centre
Ramat-Yishay 30095

Japan
Insectivorous Plant Society
Department of Biology
Nippon Dental University
Fujimi-Chiyoda-ku
Tokyo 102

United States of America
Bay Area Carnivorous Plant Society
39011 Applegate Terrace
Fremont
California CA 94536

International Carnivorous Plant Society
The Fullerton Arboretum
California State University
Fullerton CA 92634

Tampa Bay Carnivorous Plant Club
4202 E.Fowler Avenue USF 3108
Tampa, Florida 33620

Los Angeles Carnivorous Plant Society
PO Box 12281
Glendale
CA 91224-0981

Appendix B
Nurseries

Australia

Collector' Corner
810 Springvale Road
Keysborough
Victoria 3173
Australia

Telephone: 61 3 9798 5845
Fax: 61 3 9706 3339

Extensive range all year round.

Triffid Park
257 Perry Road
Keysborough
Victoria 3173
Australia

Telephone: 61 3 9769 1663
E-mail: triffid@dingley.net
www: http://www.dingley.net/triffid

Specialises in mail-order worldwide.
Extensive range.

Canada

Cherryhill Carnivorous Plants
23 Cherryhill Drive
Grimsby ON L3M 3B3
Canada

E-mail: ccp@vaxxine.com
www: http://www.vaxxine.com/ccphome

Mainly *Sarracenia* seeds.

Germany

The Nepenthes Nursery
Mudauer Ring 227
68259 Mannheim
Germany

Telephone: 49 621 705471
            49 621 715027
E-mail: andreas@wistuba.com
www: http://www.wistuba.com

Specialises in *Nepenthes*, *Heliamphora*, *Pinguicula* and *Cephalatus*. Will export internationally except to Australia and New Zealand.

United Kingdom

Cambrian Carnivores
17 Wimmerfield Road
Killay
Swansea SA2 7BU
Wales
United Kingdom

E-mail: carnivor@flytrap.demon.co.uk/
www: http://www.flytrap.demon.co.uk

Extensive list and can mail internationally.

United States of America

California Carnivores
7020 Trenton-Healdsburg Road
Forrestville
California 95436

Telephone: 1 707 838 1630
E-mail: califcarn@aol.com
www: http://www.californiacarnivores.com

Extensive collection (USA only)

Cook's Carnivorous Plants
PO Box 2594
Eugene
Oregon 97402

Telephone: 1 541 688 9426
E-mail: cooks@televar.com
www: http://www.televar.com/~cooks

Extensive range of plants.

Lee's Botanical Gardens
PO Box 669
La Belle Fla. 33975

Telephone: 1 941 675 8728

Large range.

Appendix C

Total listing

1. Venus fly trap

Family: Droseraceae
Genus: *Dionaea*

Botanical Name	Common Name	Distribution	Characteristics
D. muscipula	Venus fly trap	Carolina (USA)	Many varieties available

2. Sundew

KEY

Growing category		Physical form	
Te = Temperate climate	Tu = Tuberous	R = Rosetted	C = Climbing
Tr = Tropical climate	P = Pygmy	E = Erect	S = Scrambling
Su = Sub-tropical Climate	F = Fan-leaved		

Botanical Name	Common Name	Distribution	Category	Form	Characteristics
Drosera	sundew	Worldwide			Active Trap
D. acaulis		S Africa	Te.	R	Red or purple flowers
D. adelae	lance-leaved sundew	Queensland (Australia)	Tr	E	White, apricot and red flowers/lance-shaped leaves.
D. affinis		Tropical Africa	Tr	R	
D. alba		S Africa	Te	R	White or mauve flowers
D. aliciae		S Africa	Te	R	Green, yellow-green leaves
D. andersoniana	sturdy sundew	W Australia	Tu	E	Pink flowers
D. androsaceae		W Australia	P	R	Distinctive greyish-green bud
D. anglica	great or English sundew	Europe, USA, Japan	Te	R	4 varieties Spoon-shaped leaves
D. arcturi	alpine sundew	S Australia, NZ	Te	E	White or cream flowers
D. arenicola		Venezuela	Tr		
D. banksii	Bank's sundew	N Australia, PNG	Tr	E	
D. barbigera	Drummond's sundew	W Australia	P	R	Red flower
D. bequaertii		Central Africa	Tr	E	Pink flowers
D. biflora		Venezuela	Tr		
D. binata	forked sundew	Australia	Te	E	Forked leaves/6 varieties, white or pink flower
D. brevicornis		N Australia	Tu	R	Pink with white flowers
D. brevifolia		Brazil, Uruguay,	Te	R	Lilac or pink flowers Annual/4 varieties
D. broomensis		NW Australia	Tr	R	Pink or white flowers
D. browniana		W Australia			
D. bulbigena	midget sundew	W Australia	Tu	E	White flower
D. bulbosa	red-leaved sundew	W Australia	Tu	R	4 varieties

Botanical Name	Common Name	Distribution	Category	Form	Characteristics
D. burkeana		S Africa	Te	R	
D. burmanni	tropical sundew	N Australia, India, Asia, Papua New Guinea	Tr/Su	R	Annual/5 variations
D. cadauca		NW Australia	Tr	R	White flowers
D. callistos		W Australia	P	R	Orange flowers
D. capensis	Cape sundew	S Africa	Te	R	Ribbon-shaped leaves Narrow, pink, wide, red leaf
D. capilllaris	pink sundew	Brazil, Florida (USA)	Te	R	2 sub-species
D. cayennansis		Guyana, Brazil, Venezuela	Su	E	
D. cendeenis		Venezuela	Su	R	Mountain dweller
D. chrysolepis		Brazil	Su	E	
D. cistiflora	cistus flowered sundew	S Africa	Te	E	Large pink, white, yellow or red flowers
D. citrina		W Australia			
D. closterostigma		W Australia	P	R	White or pink flowers
D. collinsiae		S Africa	Tr	E	
D. colombiana		Colombia	Tr	R	
D. communis		Paraguay, Brazil, Cuba, Colombia	Su	R	4 variations
D. cuneifolia		South Africa	Te	R	2 variations
D. darwinensis		Australia	Tr	R	White or pink flowers
D. derbyensis		Australia	Tr	R	White flowers
D. dichrosepala	rusty sundew	West Australia	P	R	Pink or white flowers
D. dielsiana		South Africa	Te	R	Pink, mauve, violet, white flowers
D. dilatato-petiolaris		Australia	Tr	R	Purplish-pink or white flowers
D. echinoblastus		W Australia	P	R	Orange flowers
D. elongata		Angola	Tr	E/C	Up to 90 cm long
D. eneabba		W Australia	P	R	White or pink flowers
D. enodes		W Australia	P	R	pink, white flowers
D. ericksoniae		W Australia	P	R	pink, white flowers
D. erythrogyna	red ink sundew	W Australia	Tu	C	7 variations
D. erythrorhiza		W Australia	Tu	R	7 varieties
D. esmeraldae		Venezuela, Colombia	Su	R	Lilac flowers
D. falconeri		N Australia	Tr	R	Red, green kidney-shaped leaves
D. felix		Venezuela	Tr	R	
D. filiformis	thread leaf sundew	USA	Te	E	Thread-like leaves, 2 sub-species
D. fimbriata		W Australia	Tu	F	White flowers
D. fulva		N Australia	Tr	R	White or pink flowers
D. gigantea	giant sundew	W Australia	Tu	E	green, dark-red or orange-grey plant up to 100 cm
D. glabripes		S Africa	Te	E	Magenta flowers
D. glanduligera	scarlet sundew	S Australia	Te	R	Red flowers
D. graminifolia		Brazil	Tr	E	Thread-like leaves
D. graniticola		W Australia	Tu	E	White flowers
D. graomogolensis		Brazil			
D. grievei		W Australia	P	R	White flowers
D. hamiltonii	rosy sundew	W Australia	Te	R	Pink flowers

Botanical name	Common name	Distribution	Category	Form	Characteristics
D. helodes		W Australia	P	R	Pink flowers
D. heterophylla	swamp rainbow	W Australia	Tu	E	White or pink flowers
D. hilaris		S Africa	Te	R	Magenta or red/purple flowers
D. huegelii	bold sundew	West Australia	Tu	E	Purplish-pink flowers
D. humbertii		Madagascar	Tr	E	
D. hyperostigma		West Australia	P	R	Orange flowers
D. indica	Indian sundew	Australia, Asia	Tr	E	Annual, 10 varieties
D. intermedia	love nest sundew	Brazil, Carolina, S Alabama (USA)	Te	E	Spoon-shaped leaves, 6 varieties
D. insolita		Zaire	Tr	E	
D. kaieteurensis		Guyana, Trinidad, Venezuela	Tr	E	
D. katangensis		Central Africa	Tr	E	
D. kenneallyi		Australia	Tr	R	
D. lanata		Australia	Tr	R	White flowers
D. lasiantha		W Australia	P	R	
D. leucoblasta	wheel sundew	W Australia	P	R	Red or pink flowers
D. linearis		USA	Te	E	
D. lowriei		W Australia	Tu	R	5 varieties
D. macrantha	climbing sundew	S Australia	Tu	C	3 sub-species
D. macrophylla	snowy sundew	W Australia	Tu	R	3 sub-species
D. madagascariensis		Madagascar	Tr	E	Annual, pink flowers
D. mannii		W Australia	P	R	Large red flowers
D. marchantii		W Australia	Tu	E	2 variations
D. menziesii	pink rainbow	W Australia	Tu	C	5 sub-species
D. meristocaulis		Venezuela	Tr	E	Narrow leaves, white flowers
D. microphylla	purple rainbow	W Australia	Tu	E	2 variations, pink or purple flowers
D. miniata		W Australia	P	R	Orange flowers
D. modesta	modest rainbow	W Australia	Tu	C	White flowers
D. montana		Brazil, Venezuela	Su	R	11 variations
D. myriantha	star rainbow	W Australia	Tu	E	White flowers
D. natalensis		S Africa	Te	R	Spoon-shaped leaves, pink flowers
D. neesii	jewel rainbow	W Australia	Tu	E	3 sub-species
D. neo-caledonica		New Caledonia	Tr	R	Annual, long narrow leaves
D. nitidula	shining sundew	West Australia	P	R	4 sub-species
D. oblanceolata		China	Te	R	
D. occidentalis	western rainbow	West Australia	P	R	4 variations
D. orbiculata		West Australia	Tu	R	White flowers
D. ordensis		North West Australia	Su	R	Pink to white flowers
D. oreopodion		West Australia	P	R	White flowers
D. paleacea	dwarf sundew	West Australia	P	R	2 sub-species
D. pallida	pale rainbow	West Australia	Tu	C	White flower
D. panamensis		Panama	Te	R	Annual
D. parvula	cone sundew	West Australia	P	R	White flowers
D. paradoxa		North Australia	Tr	E	Pink or white flowers, 30 cm tall
D. pauciflora		South Africa	Te	R	White, yellow, pink flowers
D. peltata	pale sundew	Australia	Tu	E	6 sub-species
D. petiolaris	woolly sundew	Northern Australia	Tr	R	5 variations
D. pilosa		Cameroon, Kenya	Te	R	Red or reddish-purple flowers
D. platypoda	fan-leaved sundew	West Australia	Tu	F	White flowers

Botanical name	Common name	Distribution	Category	Form	Characteristics
D. platystigma	black-eyed sundew	W Australia	P	R	Red flowers
D. prolifera	trailing sundew	Queensland	Tr	S	Kidney shaped leaves
D. prostratoscaposa		W Australia	Te		
D. pulchella	pretty sundew	W Australia	P	R	13 variations
D. pycnoblasta	pearly sundew	W Australia	P	R	White flowers
D. pygmaea	pygmy sundew	Australia	P	R	3 variations
D. radicans		W Australia	Tu	E	White flowers
D. ramellosa	branched sundew	W Australia	Tu	F	White or pink flowers
D. ramentacea		S Africa	Te.	E	Magenta flowers
D. rechingeri		W Australia	P	R	Yellow with white flowers
D. regia		S Africa	Te	R	Pink or purple flowers, narrow but large leaves
D. roraimae		Venezuela	Tr	R	
D. rosulata		W Australia	Te	R	White flowers
D. rotundifolia	round-leaved sundew	Czech, USA, Canada	Te	R	13 variations
D. salina		W Australia	Tu	E	White flowers
D. sargentii		W Australia	P	R	White flowers
D. schizandra	notched sundew	Queensland	Tr	E	Large broad leaves
D. scorpioides	shaggy sundew	W Australia	P	R	Pink or white flower
D. sessilifolia		Brazil, Guyana, Venezuela	Su	R	Annual, pink flowers
D. sewelliae		W Australia	P	R	Orange flowers
D. silvicola		W Australia	P	R	
D. slackii		S Africa	Te	R	
D. spathulata	spoon leaf sundew	Australia, NZ, Asia	Te	R	13 variations
D. spilos		W Australia	P	R	Pink, white flowers
D. stenopetala		New Zealand	Te	R	
D. stolonifera	leafy sundew	W Australia	Tu	F	7 sub-species
D. stricticaulis	erect sundew	W Australia	Tu	E	2 variations
D. subhirtella	sunny rainbow	W Australia	Tu	C, S	2 sub-species, yellow flowers
D. subtilis		N Australia	Su	E	White or yellow flowers
D. trinervia		S Africa	Te	R	9 variations
D. tubaestylis		W Australia	Tu	R	2 variations
D. uniflora		China, Argnetina	Su	R	Purple flowers
D. villosa		Brazil	Su	R	3 variations
D. walyunga		W Australia	P	R	White or pink flowers
D. whittakeri	scented sundew	S Australia	Tu	R	2 variations
D. zonaria	painted sundew	W Australia	Tu	R	Kidney shaped leaves

3. Rainbow plant

Botanical Name	Common Name	Distribution	Characteristics
Byblis	rainbow plant	Australia, Papua New Guinea	Passive flypaper trap
B. aquatica		Northern Territory	Purple flowers
B. filifolia		Western Australia, Northern Territory	Mauve flowers withwhite, yellow, or yellow with mauve stripes underneath
B. gigantea		Western Australia	Lilac flowers
B. liniflora		Western Australia, Northern Territory	Pinkish mauve flowers with white underneath
B. rorida		Western Australia	Mauve flowers with white underneath

89

4. Waterwheel plant

Family: Droseraceae
Genus: Alvrovanda

Botanical Name	Common Name	Distribution	Characteristics
A. vesiculosa	waterwheel plant	Europe, Africa, India, Japan, Australia	Aquatic species

5. Pitcher plant

Botanical Name	Common name	Distribution	Flower	Forms And Varieties
Sarracenia	pitcher plants	USA		Passive pitchers
S. alata	pale pitcher plant	SE USA	White to yellow	Forms (green/red throat/*pubescens*)
S. flava	yellow trumpet	SE USA	Yellow	Variations (*maxima*—green from Carolina coast, *ornata*—heavily veined, *rugelli*, copper lid, Marston dwarf, red)
S. leucophylla	white trumpet	SE USA	Burgundy	Forms(short pitcher, red veins/green veins, yellow flower)
S. minor	hooded pitcher plant	SE USA	Yellow	
S. oreophila	green pitcher plant	SE USA	Yellowish-green	
S. psittacina	parrot pitcher	SE USA	Red	Prostrate plant
S. purpurea	purple pitcher plant	E USA	Green, pink or burgundy	Prostrate, sub-species/Canada (*purpurea*—long and narrow, *venosa*—filled hood, short and fat)
S. rubra	sweet trumpet	SE USA	Red	Sub-species (*rubra, alabamensis, gulensis, jonesii, wherryi*)

Some common hybrids

Name	Species contained within hybrid	Name	Species contained within hybrid
aerolata	alata × leucophylla	minata	alata × minor
catesbaei	flava × purpurea ssp. venosa	mitchelliana	leucophylla × purpurea
chelsonii	purpurea × rubra	moorei	flava × leucophylla
courtii	psittacina × purpurea	popei	flava × rubra
excellens	leucophylla × minor	readii	leucophylla × rubra
exornata	alata × purpurea	rehderii	minor × rubra
formosa	minor × psittacina	swaniana	minor × purpurea
gilpini	psittacina × rubra	wrigleyana	leucophylla × psittacina
harperi	flava × minor		

6. Cobra lily

Family: Sarraceniaceae
Genus: Darlingtonia

Botanical Name	Common Name	Distribution	Characteristics
D. californica	cobra lily	Oregon to northern California (USA)	Crimson flowers

7. *Sun pitcher*

Botanical Name	Distribution	Characteristics
Heliamphora	Venezuela	Passive Trap
H. heterodoxa	Mt Ptari-Tepui, Venezuela	Variations: *heterodoxa, exappendiculata, glabra*
H. ionasi	Ilu-tepui, Venezuela	
H. minor	Mt Auyan-Tepui, Venezuela	
H. neblinae	Cerro de la Neblina, Venezuela	Variations: *neblinae*—white flowers, *parva*—shorter, pitchers, red and white sepals with pale pink, *viridis*—greenish flowers
H. nutans	Mt Roraima, Venezuela	
H. tatei	Mt Duida, Venezuela	Variations: *tatei, macdonaldae, neblinae*

8. *Albany pitcher plant*

Botanical Name	Common Name	Distribution	Characteristics
C. follicularis	Albany pitcher plant	West Australia (south-west)	Passive trap

9. *Tropical pitcher plant*

Family: Nepenthaceae

H= Highland   L=Lowland   C=Climbing   S=Scrambling
na = information not available

Botanical Name	Common Name	Distribution	Altitude	Type	Pitcher (cm)	Max Ht (m)	Characteristics
Nepenthes	tropical pitcher plant	SE Asia, Australia, Madagascar, India					
N. adnata		Sumatra	H	na	na	na	
N. alata	winged nepenthes	Philippines, Malaysia, Sumatra	H/L	C	25	4	
N. albo-marginata	white-collared	Borneo, Sumatra	L	C	20	2	White stripe on rim, green or purple pitchers
N. ampullaria	phial nepenthes	Borneo, PNG, Singapore, Sumatra	L	S	10	2	
N. anamensis		Thailand and Cambodia to Vietnam	H	na	na	na	
N. argentii		Philippines	H	S	4	0.3	
N. aristolochioides		Sumatra	H	C	9	na	Unusual bladder shaped pitchers
N. bellii		Philippines	L	na	na	na	
N. bicalarata	fanged pitcher plant	Borneo	L	C	18	15	Produces two fangs
N. bongso		Sumatra	H	C/S	13	2	
N. borneensis	Borneo pitcher plant	Borneo	H	C	17	na	
N. boshiana	Bosch's pitcher plant	Borneo	H	C	25	na	
N. burbidgeae	Burbidge's pitcher plant	Borneo	H	C	25	10	
N. burkei		Philippines	H	na	na	na	
N. campanulata	bell-shaped pitcher plant	Borneo	L	C	7	35 cm	

Botanical Name	Common Name	Distribution	Altitude	Type	Pitcher (cm)	Max Ht (m)	Characteristics
N. carunculata		Sumatra	H	C	17	na	
N. clipeata	shield-leaved pitcher	Borneo	H	S	30	50 cm	Round leaves. Plant covered with long brown hairs
N. danseri		New Guinea, Moluccas	L	C/S	10	4	
N. densiflora		Sumatra	H	na	na	na	
N. diatas		Sumatra	H	S	22	2.5	
N. distillatoria		Sri Lanka	L	na	na	na	
N. dubia		Sumatra	H	na	na	na	
N. edwardsiana	splendid pitcher plant	Borneo	H	C	35	15	Described as most beautiful and spectacular
N. ephippiata	saddle-leaved pitcher plant	Borneo	H	C	15	3	
N. eustachya		Sumatra	H	C	11	5	
N. eymae		Sulawesi	H	C	11	na	
N. fusca	dusky pitcher plant	Borneo	H	S	18	10	
N. glabrata		Sulawesi	H	na	na	na	
N. gracilis	slender pitcher plant	Borneo, Sumatra, Thailand, Singapore, Sulawesi	L	C	15	10	Widespread and common species
N. gracillima		Malaysia, Sumatra	H	C	23	5	
N. gynamphora		Borneo, Sumatra, Java	H	C	18	15	
N. hamata		Sulawesi	H	na	na	na	
N. hirsuta	hairy pitcher plant	Borneo	H	C	15	2	
N. hispida		Borneo	L	C	12	6	
N. inermis		Sumatra	H	C	9	na	
N. insignis		New Guinea	L	C	16	80 cm	
N. khasiana		India	H		17	2	Recommended for cooler climates
N. klossii		New Guinea	H	C	18	2	
N. lamii		New Guinea	H	C/S	11	na	
N. lowii	Low's pitcher plant	Borneo	H	C/E	28	10	Unusual shaped upper pitchers
N. macfarlanei		Malaysia	H	C	20	3	
N. macrophylla	large-leaved pitcher plant	Borneo	H	C	35	na	
N. macrovulgaris	serpentine pitcher plant	Borneo	L	C	23	6	Pitchers range from green to dark brown
N. madagascariensis		Madagascar	H	na	na	na	
N. mapuluensis	Mapulu pitcher plant	Borneo	L	na	21	na	
N. masoalensis		Madagascar	L	na	na	na	
N. maxima	great pitcher plant	Borneo, Sulawesi, New Guinea	H	C	30	na	
N. merilliana		Philippines	L	S/C	20	na	
N. mikea		Sumatra	H	na	13	na	
N. mirabilis	common swamp	Asia, New Guuinea, Australia	L	C	20	7	Widespread distribution
N. mollis	velvet pitcher plant	Borneo	H	C	na	na	

Botanical Name	Common Name	Distribution	Altitude	Type	Pitcher (cm)	Max Ht (m)	Characteristics
N. muluensis	mulu pitcher plant	Borneo	H	S	10	1.5	
N. murudensis	murud pitcher plant	Borneo	H	S	6	1.5	
N. neo-guineensis		New Guinea	L	C	na	na	
N. northiana	Miss North's pitcher plant	Borneo	L	C	40	3	
N. ovata		Sumatra	H	C	na	na	
N. paniculata		New Guinea	H	C	11	7	
N. papuana		New Guinea	L	C	6	na	
N. pectinata		Sumatra	H	C	16	4	
N. pervillei		Seychelles	L	C	na	na	
N. petiolata		Philippines	L	na	na	na	
N. pilosa	golden-furred pitcher plant	Borneo	H	C	28	7	
N. rafflesiana	Raffle's pitcher plant	Sumatra,Borneo	L	S	35	10	
N. rafflesiana elegans		Sumatra, Borneo	L	S	35	10	
N. rajah	Rajah Brooke's	Borneo	H	S	50	5	The largest pitchers
N. ramispina		Malaysia	H	C	18	5	
N. reinwardtiana	Reinwardt's pitcher plant	Borneo, Malaysia, Sumatra	L	C	23	10	
N. rhombicaulis		Sumatra	H	na	na	na	
N. sanguinea		Malaysia	H	C	30	7	
N. singalana		Sumatra	H	C	20	na	
N. spathulata		Sumatra	H	na	na	na	
N. spectabilis		Sumatra	H	C	26	6	
N. stenophylla	narrow-leaved pitcher plant	Borneo	H	C	25	6	
N. sumatrana		Sumatra	L	C	23	3	
N. tentaculata	fringed pitcher plant	Borneo, Sulawesi, New Guinea	H	C	15	2	
N. thorelii		Indo China	L	S	12	0.4	
N. tobaica		Sumatra	H	C	9	5	
N. tomoriana		Sulawesi	L	C	13	na	
N. treubiana		New Guinea	H	C	23	na	
N. truncata		Philippines	L	na	na	na	
N. veitchii	Veitch's pitcher plant	Borneo	H	C	32	10	Ability to climb trees
N. ventricosa		Phillipines	H	na	15	2	
N. vieillardii		New Caledonia, New Guinea	H	C	14	na	
N. villosa	hairy nepenthes	Borneo	H	S	25	2	

Common Nepenthes hybrids

Name	Species contained within hybrid	Name	Species contained within hybrid
allardii	*maxima* × *veitchii*	*maria-louisa*	*maxima* × *northiana*
alliotii	*maxima* × *northiana*	*masahiroi*	*albo-marginata* × *thorelii*
cincta	*albo-marginata* × *northiana*	*masamiae*	*maxima* × *thorelii*
dicksoniana	*rafflesiana* × *veitchii*	*mastersiana*	*khasiana* × *sanguinea*
dominii	*gracilis* × *rafflesiana*	*mercieri*	*maxima* × *northiana*
emmarene	*khasiana* × *ventricosa*	*mixta*	*maxima* × *northiana*
excelsa	*sanguinea* × *veitchii*	*nakanogo*	*mirabilis* × *rafflesiana*
fournieri	*maxima* × *northiana*	*nobilis*	*maxima* 'superba' × *sanguinea*
grandis	*maxima* 'superba' × *northiana* 'pulchra'	*rokko*	*maxima* × *thorelii*
		sedenii	*gracilis* × *khasiana*
harryana	*edwardsiana* × *villosa*	*simonii*	*maxima* × *northiana*
hookerae	*mirabilis* × *rafflesiana*	*tiveyi*	*maxima* 'superba' × *veitchii*
hookeriana	*ampullaria* × *rafflesiana*	*toyoshimae*	*thorelii* × *truncata*
hybrida	*gracilis* × *khasiana*	*trichocarpa*	*ampullaria* × *gracilis*
intermedia	*gracilis* × *rafflesiana*	*trusmadiensis*	*edwardsiana* × *lowii*
issey	*alata* × *burkei*	*ventrata*	*alata* × *ventricosa*
kinabaluensis	*rajah* × *villosa*	*wittei*	*maxima* × *stenophylla*
kuchingensis	*ampullaria* × *mirabilis*	*yatomi*	*thorelii* × *veitchii*
lecouflei	*mirabilis* × *thorelli*	*yoyogi*	*deaniana* × *ventricosa*

10. Butterwort

KEY

Climate

Tr = Tropical   Su = Sub-tropical

Te = Terrestrial

Leaf form

A = One leaf form   H = Forms winter dormancy bud

B = Two leaf forms

Botanical Name	Distribution	Climate	Leaf Forms	Flower
Pinguicula	Worldwide			
P. acuminata	Mexico	Tr	B	White
P. agnata	Mexico	Tr	A	White with purple rim
P. albida	Cuba	Tr	A	
P. algida	Siberia	Te	A/H	
P. alpina	Europe, Asia	Te	A/H	White with yellow spots
P. antarctica	Chile, Argentina, Peru	Tr	A	
P. balcanica	Bulgaria, Yugoslavia, Albania, Greece	Te	B	Purple
P. barbata	Mexico	Tr	A	
P. benedicta	Cuba	Tr	A	
P. caerulea	USA	Su	A	
P. calyprata	Colombia, Ecuador	Tr	A	
P. casabitoana	Cuba	Tr	A	
P. chilensis	Chile, Argentina	Tr	A	
P. colimensis	Mexico	Tr	B	
P. corsica	Corsica	Te	A/H	White
P. crassifolia	Mexico	Tr	B	
P. crenatiloba	Mexico, Guatemala, Honduras, El Salvador, Panama	Tr	A	
P. crystallina	Cyprus	Tr	A	White
P. cyclosecta	Mexico	Tr	B	Magenta
P. debbertiana	Mexico	Tr	B	
P. ehlersae	Mexico	Tr	B	Magenta with white centre
P. elongata	Venezuela, Colombia	Tr	B	

Botanical Name	Distribution	Climate	Leaf Forms	Flower
P. emarginata	Mexico	Tr	A	Purple and white
P. esseriana	Mexico	Tr	B	Mauve with yellow centre or white with purple nerves
P. filifolia	Cuba	Tr	A	
P. gracilis	Mexico	Tr	A	
P. grandiflora	France, Switzerland, Spain, Ireland, England	Te	A/H	Purple
P. greenwoodii	Mexico	Tr		
P. gypsicola	Mexico	Tr	B	Pink or purple with pale on rear
P. hemiepiphytica	Mexico	Tr	B	Pink with white
P. heterophylla	Mexico	Tr	B	
P. imitatrix	Mexico	Tr	B	
P. immaculata	Mexico	Tr	A	
P. involuta	Bolivia, Peru	Tr	A	
P. ionantha	Florida	Su	A	
P. jackii	Cuba	Tr	A	
P. jaumavensis	Mexico	Tr	B	Pink with yellow
P. kondoi	Mexico	Tr	B	
P. laueana	Mexico	Tr	B	Red
P. laxifolia	Mexico	Tr		Pink or violet
P. leptoceras	Switzerland, Austria, Italy, France	Te	A/H	Purple or pink with white
P. lignicola	Cuba	Tr	A	
P. lilacina	Mexico	Tr	A	
P. longifolia	Spain, France, Italy	Te	B	Purple with white
P. lusitanica	Portugal, France, England, N Africa, Spain	Te	A	White
P. lutea	USA	Su	A	
P. macroceras	Japan, Russia, Nth America	Te	A/H	Mauve with white
P. macrophylla	Mexico	Tr	B/H	Purple with white spot
P. mirandea	Mexico	Tr		
P. moctezumea	Mexico	Tr		Pink with white
P. moranensis	Mexico, Guatamala, El Salvador	Tr	B	Pink
P. nevadensis	Spain	Te	A/H	White
P. oblongiloba	Mexico	Tr	B/H	
P. orchidioides	Mexico	Tr		Magenta or white
P. parvifolia	Mexico	Tr	B/H	
P. planifolia	USA	Su	A	
P. potosiensis	Mexico	Tr	B	Purple
P. primuliflora	USA	Su	A	Purple with white
P. pumila	USA	Su	A	
P. ramosa	Japan	Te	A/H	White with purple
P. rectifolia	Mexico	Tr	B	
P. reticulata	Mexico	Tr	B	White with purple
P. rotundiflora	Mexico	Tr	B	
P. sharpii	Mexico	Tr	A	
P. takakii	Mexico	Tr	A	
P. utricularioides	Mexico	Tr	B	
P. vallisneriifolia	Spain	Tr	B	Purple with white
P. variegata	Siberia	Te	A/H	Purple with white
P. villosa	Alaska, Canada, Norway, Finland, Russia	Te	A/H	Purple
P. vulgaris	Europe, Siberia, Canada, Nth USA	Te	A/H	Pink with white
P. zecheri	Mexico	Tr	B	Pink

11. *Bladderwort*

KEYS

Habitat		*Climate*
T = Terrestrial	R = Rheophytes	Tr = Tropical
A = Aquatic	L = Lithophytes	Su = Subtropical
E = Epiphytic		Te = Temperate

Botanical Name	Common Name	Distribution	Habitat	Climate	Flower	Stem (cm)
Utricularia	Bladderwort	Worldwide				
U. adpressa		S America	T	Su	Yellow	18
U. albiflora		Australia	T	Tr	White	4.
U. albocaerulea		India	T	Su	Blue	15
U. alpina	alpine bladderwort	West Indies, C & S America	E	Su	White	30
U. amethystina		C, N & S America	T	Su	Violet or mauve (yellow spot)	30
U. andongensis		Eastern & Southern Africa	T	Tr	Yellow	20
U. antennifera		West Australia	T	Te	Apricot	12
U. appendiculata		Central Africa, Madagascar	T	Tr	White/cream/ yellow	60
U. arnhemica		Australia	A/T	Tr	Violet with yellow or white blotch	30
U. arcuata		India	T	Su	Blue-violet	20
U. arenaria		Central & Southern, Africa, India	T	Tr	White, lilac or violet	20
U. asplundii		Ecuador, Columbia	E/T	Tr	White	36
U. aurea	golden bladderwort	Australia, Asia	A	Te/Su	Yellow	25
U. aureomaculata		Venezuela (mountains)	L	Tr	Yellow with orange spot	25
U. australis	yellow bladderwort	Australia, Japan, Europe, NZ, Asia	A	Te	Yellow	30–90
U. benjaminiana		West Indies, Suriname, Tropical Africa	A	Su	Mauve with yellow blotch at base	25
U. benthamii		West Australia	T	Te	Purple or white	7–13
U. bifida	winged bladderwort	Australia, India, Japan	T	Tr	Yellow	20
U. biloba	moth bladderwort	Australia, SE Asia, PNG	T	Su	Blue	45
U. biovularioides		Brazil	A	Tr	White	12mm
U. bisquamata		Madagascar, S Africa	T	Su	Lilac, violet, yellow or white with yellow at base	2.5
U. blanchettii		Brazil	T, L	Tr	Purple with orange-yellow blotch	15
U. bosminifera		Thailand	T	Tr	Yellow	15
U. brachiata		India (mountains)	L	Te	White with yellow spot	8
U. bracteata		Africa	T	Tr	Yellow	30
U. bremii		Europe	A	Te	Yellow	50
U. breviscapa		Cuba, Guyana Suriname	A	Su	Yellow with reddish brown marks at base	10
U. buntingiana		Venezuela	E	Su	Lavender or mauve with yellow at base	8
U. caerulea	blue bladderwort	Australia, India, Japan	T	Su	White, yellow, pink or violet	30
U. calycifida		Venezuela, Guyana, Suriname	T	Su	Lavender with yellow blotch or wholly white yellow or brown	10

Botanical Name	Common Name	Distribution	Habitat	Climate	Flower	Stem (cm)
U. campbelliana		Venezuela, Guyana (mts)	E	Su	Orange–red with yellow at base	13
U. cappilliflora	hairflower bladderwort	Australia	T	Tr	Flesh tone	12
U. cecilii		India	T	Su	Violet with white patch	17
U. cheiranthos		Australia	T	Tr	Pink with yellow at base	3
U. chiribiquitensis		Colombia, Venezuela	T	Tr	Yellow	30
U. choristotheca		Suriname	R	Su	Ochre yellow with red	2.5
U. christopheri		Nepal (mts)	L	Te	White with yellow spot	4
U. chrysantha		Australia, PNG (3 varieties)	T	Tr	Yellow with orange or brown spots	60
U. circumvoluta		Australia	T	Tr	Yellow	40
U. corynephora		Burma, Thailand	L	Tr	Mauve with yellow spot	10
U. cornuta		USA, Bahamas, Cuba	T	Te	Yellow	40
U. costata		Venezuela	T	Su	Lavender or violet with yellow blotch	7
U. cucullata		South America	A	Su	Pink with white or yellow spots	10
U. cymbantha		South Africa	A	Tr, Te	White or cream	1.5
U. delicatula		New Zealand	T	Te	Lavender	15
U. delphinioides		SE Asia	T	Tr	Purple	60
U. determannii		Sth America	R	Su	White with purple and yellow blotch	2.5
U. dichotoma	fairy aprons	Australia	T	Te	Violet with yellow at the base	50
U. dimorphantha		Japan	A	Te	Yellow	10
U. dunlopii		Australia	T	Tr	Flesh tone	12
U. dunstaniae	thread-flower bladderwort	Australia	T	Tr	Flesh tone	15
U. endresii		Central & South America	E	Su	Lavender or lilac with yellow blotch	32
U. erectiflora		Central &South America	T	Su	Yellow	35
U. fimbriata		Colombia, Venezuela	T	Su	Yellow	30
U. firmula		Africa, Madagascar	T	Su	Yellow with orange spot	20
U. fistulosa		West Australia	A	Te	White with mauve or yellow spot	50
U. flaccida		Brazil	T	Su	Yellow	50
U. floridana		USA (Florida, Carolina)	A	Te	Yellow with red streaks	1 m
U. foliosa		USA, Africa, C & S America	A	Te	Yellow with purple	45
U. forrestii		China	L	Te	Mauve or violet	4
U. foveolata		India, Aust, SE Asia, China, Africa, Madagascar	T	Te/Tr	Mauve	20
U. fulva	spotted bladderwort	Australia	T/A	Tr	Yellow	40
U. furcellata		India	L	Te	White, violet or pink	4
U. garrettii		Thailand	L	Tr	Voilet with yellow or white spot	6
U. geminiloba		Brazil	L/T	Su	Blue-violet with yellow at base	45
U. geminiscapa		USA (NE), Canada	A	Te	Yellow	25
U. geoffrayi		SE Asia, Thailand	T	Tr	Purple, mauve or white	20
U. georgei		West Australia,	T	Te	White with some violet	17
U. gibba	floating bladderwort	Australia, USA, Japan, S America, SE Asia, Africa	A	Te/Tr	Yellow	20

Botanical Name	Common Name	Distribution	Habitat	Climate	Flower	Stem (cm)
U. graminifolia		India, Ceylon, Burma, Thailand, China	T	Tr	Mauve or violet	30
U. guyanensis		C & S America	T	Su	Yellow	13
U. hamiltonii	pin-eared bladderwort	Australia	A	Tr	Violet with orange-yellow patch	10
U. helix		West Australia	A	Te	Mauve with yellow	35
U. heterochroma		Venezuela	R	Su	White with yellow, lavender spots	6
U. heterosepala		Philippines	A	Tr	White, pink, blue or violet	15
U. hintonii		Mexico	L	Te		
U. hirta		India & SE Asia	T	Tr	Violet, mauve or white	15
U. hispida		C & S America	T	Su	Blue, white or yellow	60
U. holtzei	fan bladderwort	Australia	T	Tr	Cream with orange spot	6
U. humboltii		Venezuela, Guyana, Brazil	A/T	Su	Blue-violet with yellow	1.3 m
U. huntii		Brazil	T	Su	Mauve with yellow blotch	40
U. hydrocarpa		USA, Cuba, Mexico	A	Su	Pink or lilac with yellow blotch	10
U. inequalis	twining bladder	Australia	T	Te	Purple	20
U. incisa		Cuba	A	Su	Yellow	18
U. inflata		SE USA	A	Te	Yellow	50
U. inflexa		Australia, Africa, India, Madagascar	A	Tr	White or yellow with purple	33
U. intermedia		USA, Europe, Asia	A	Te	Yellow	20
U. involvens		N Aust, Malaysia, Burma, Thailand	T	Tr	Yellow	60
U. jamesoniana		Central America	E	Su	White with a yellow or magenta blotch	10
U. juncea		N, C and S America, West Indies	T	Su	Yellow	45
U. kamienskii	white bladderwort	Australia	T	Tr	White or lilac with yellow at base	20
U. kenneallyii		NW Australia	T	Te	Lower lip mauve, upper lip white with mauve	13
U. kimberleyensis	Kimberley bladderwort	Australia	T	Su	Purple	25
U. kumaonensis		Himalayas	E	T	White with yellow spot	7
U. laciniata		Brazil	T	Su	Lavender with yellow spot	16
U. asiocaulis	downy bladderwort	Australia	T	Su	Violet with yellow spots	25
U. lateriflora	small bladderwort	Australia	T	Te	Mauve or violet with white or yellow spots	20
U. laxa		Argentina, Brazil, Paraguay, Uruguay	T	Su	Yellow	40
U. lazulina		India	T	Su	Blue with white patch	10
U. leptoplectra	dragonfly bladderwort	Australia	T	Tr	Violet with white spot	1 m
U. leptorhyncha	beak bladderwort	Australia	T	Tr	Violet with yellow throat	16
U. letestui		Africa	T	Tr	Yellow	22
U. limosa		Australia, SE Asia, China	T	Tr	Violet or white with yellow spot	35
U. livida		Madagascar, Mexico, East Africa	T	Su	Violet with yellow blotch	80
U. lloydii		C & S America	T	Tr	Yellow	22
U. longeciliata		Brazil, Suriname, Guyana, Venezuela, Colombia	T	Su	Yellow	35

Botanical Name	Common Name	Distribution	Habitat	Climate	Flower	Stem (cm)
U. longifolia		Brazil	T.	Su	Violet with orange-yellow blotch	60
U. machrocheilos		West Africa	T	Tr	Yellow	27
U. macrorhiza		USA, East Asia	A	T	Yellow with reddish-brown streaks	40
U. mannii		Africa	E	Tr	Yellow	9
U. menziesii	redcoats	West Australia	T	Te	Red with yellow at base	7
U. meyeri		Brazil	T	Su	Yellow	60
U. microcalyx		Central Africa	T	Tr	Violet with yellow blotch	30
U. micropetala		West Africa	T	Tr	Yellow	16
U. minor		Canada, Nth USA, Europe, Asia	A	Te	Yellow	25
U. minutissima	minute bladderwort	Australia, India, Japan, Asia	T	Tr	Purple, mauve or white	15
U. mirabilis		Venezuela	R	Tr	White	20
U. monanthos	Tasmanian bladderwort	Australia, New Zealand	T	Te	Purple with yellow at base	4
U. moniliformis		Sri Lanka	L	Su	Pale violet with violet streaks	15
U. muelleri		Nth Australia, PNG	A	Tr	Yellow with red streaks	30
U. multicaulis		China, Nepal, India	T,L	Te	White or mauve with yellow spot	5
U. multifida	pink petticoat	Western Australia	T	Te	Pink with yellow	45
U. myriocista		South America	A	Su	Pink with yellow blotch	10
U. nana		Brazil, Guyana, Suriname, Venezuela, Paraguay	T	Su	Yellow	6
U. naviculata		Brazil, Venezuela	A	Tr	White	5
U. nelumbifolia		Brazil	A	Tr	Blue-violet	1.2 m
U. neottioides		Brazil, Colombia, Venezuela, Bolivia	R	Su	Cream or greenish-white with yellow spot	30
U. nephrophylla		Brazil	L	Tr	White or mauve with yellow	35
U. nervosa		South America	T	Su	Orange-yellow	50
U.sp'New Zealand		New Zealand	T	Te.	Violet	30
U. nigrescens		Brazil	T	Tr	Yellow	20
U. novae-zelandiae		New Zealand, New Caledonia	T	Te	White with violet and yellow	10
U. ochroleuca		Europe, NW USA	A	Te	Yellow	15
U. odontosepala		Malawi, Zambia, Zaire	T	A	Mauve or violet with yellow blotch	30
U. odorata		Australia, SE Asia	T	Tr	Orange-yellow	55
U. olivacea		North, C and S America	A	Te	Creamy-white	2
U. oliveriana		Venezuela, Colombia, Brazil	R	Su	White	9
U. panamensis		Panama	L	Te	Lavender with white and yellow	17
U. parthenopipes		Brazil	T	Su	White with orange-yellow spot	22
U. pentadactyla		Eastern Africa	T	Tr	Mauve to white with yellow spot	30
U. peranomala		China	L	Te	Yellow	2.5
U. perversa		Mexico	A	Te	Yellow	12
U. petersoniae		Mexico	L	Su	Violet with yellow blotch	7
U. physoceras		Brazil	T	Su	Red, lilac or white	20
U. pierrei		Vietnam, Cambodia, Thailand	T	Tr	Yellow	30

Botanical Name	Common Name	Distribution	Habitat	Climate	Flower	Stem (cm)
U. platensis		Argentina, Uruguay, Brazil, Paraguay	A	Su	Yellow	22
U. pobeguinii		Africa	T	Te	Blue with white patch	20
U. poconensis		Argentina, Brazil	A	Su	White or violet	25
U. podadena		Mozambique, Malawi	T	Te	Yellow	24
U. polygaloides		India, Ceylon	T	Su	Violet	20
U. praelonga		Brazil, Paraguay, Argentina	T	Su	Yellow	60
U. praeterita		India	T	Su	Violet	15
U. praetermissa		Central America	E,T	Su	White or pink with yellow	45
U. prehensilis		East Africa, Angola, Brazil, Paraguay	T	Su	Yellow	35
U. pubescens		Africa, Venezuela, Guyana, India, Brazil	T	Tr	Violet or lilac with yellow blotch	35
U. pulchra		Papua New Guinea	T/L	Tr	Mauve or violet with yellow spot	6
U. punctata		Burma, Thailand, Borneo	A	Tr	Lilac, violet, pink or white with yellow blotch	30
U. purpurea		USA, Cuba, Canada	A	Te	Pink with yellow blotch	20
U. purpureocaerulea		Brazil	T	Su	Lavender or violet	16
U. pusilla		Central and South America	T	Su	Yellow	20
U. quelchii		Venezuela, Brazil (mts)	E/T	Su	Red with yellow blotch	20
U. quinquedentata		Nth Australia	T	Su	White with yellow spot	5
U. radiata		USA, Canada	A	Te	Yellow with brown	25
U. raynalii		Tropical and Central Africa	A	Tr/Su	Pink or purple with yellow blotch	2
U. recta		India, Nepal, China(mts)	T	Te	Yellow	20
U. reflexa		Madagascar, West Africa	A	Te	Yellow with brown or purple spots	18
U. reniformis		Brazil	E	Su		
U. resupinata		East Canada, East USA, S America	A	Te	Pink with cream spot	20
U. reticulata		India, Ceylon	T	Su	Violet with with patch	1 m
U. rhododactylos		N Australia	T	Tr	Mauve with yellow, white margined patch	7
U. rigida		West Africa	R	Tr	White or yellow with dark yellow spot	35
U. salwinensis		China	T/L	Te	White or pink with yellow spot	7mm
U. sandersonii		South Africa	L	Te	White or mauve with dark mauve blotch	6
U. sandwithii		Guyana, Brazil, Venezuela, Surinam	T/L	Su	Purple with orange-yellow blotch	15
U. scandens	tall bladderwort	Africa, Asia	T	Tr	Yellow	35
U. schultesii		Colombia, Venezuela	T	Su	White or violet	18
U. simplex	bluecoats	Australia	T	Te	Lilac with yellow spot	5
U. simulans		Central Africa, S America	T	Su	Yellow	35
U. singeriana	showy bladderwort	Australia	T	Tr	Purple, mauve or violet	30
U. smithiana		India	T	Tr	Mauve or violet	50
U. spiralis		Central Africa	T	Tr	Violet with yellow blotch	70
U. spruceana		Brazil, Venezuela	T	Su	White or lavender with yellow patch	5
U. stanfieldii		West Africa	T	Tr	Yellow	16

Botanical Name	Common Name	Distribution	Habitat	Climate	Flower	Stem (cm)
U. steenisii		Sumatra	T/L	Tr	White with yellow spot	7
U. stellaris	star bladderwort	Africa, Asia, India, Australia	A	Tr	Yellow	30
U. steyermarkii		Venezuela	L	Su	Yellow	12
U. striata		USA	A	Te	Yellow with red streaks	40
U. striatula		Asia, Central Africa, New Guinea	E/L	Tr	White with violet and yellow spot	20
U. subulata		Americas, Africa, Madagascar, Australia, Asia, India	T.	Te/Su	Yellow, white or red	50
U. tenella	pinkfan	Southern Australia	T	Te	Pink with yellow	13
U. tenuissima		South America (North)	T	Su	Violet, mauve or white with yellow blotch	8
U. terrae-reginae		Australia	T	Su	White or violet with dark violet streaks	17
U. tetraloba		West Africa	R	Tr	White with yellow patch	7
U. tortilis		Africa	T	Tr	Violet with blue, yellow or white spot	40
U. trichophylla		Central & South America	A/T	Su	Yellow	30
U. tricolor		Brazil, Paraguay, Colombia, Venezuela, Argentina	T	Su	Violet and lilac with white and yellow at base	60
U. tridactyla		West Australia	T	Su	Violet with 2 yellow ridges	20
U. tridentata		Brazil, Uruguay, Argentina	T	Su	Violet or lavender with white or yellow at base	22
U. triflora		Northern Australia	T	Tr	Mauve with cream, pruple blotch	14
U. triloba		Central & South America	T	Su	Yellow	30
U. troupinii		Central Africa	T	Tr	Yellow	18
U. tubulata	bloated bladderwort	Australia	A	Tr	Pink with yellowish-white and violet	37
U. uliginosa	Asia bladderwort	Asia, Australia	T	Su	Lilac or violet with white	30
U. uniflora		Australia	T	Te	Mauve or lilac with yellow and white	20
U. unifolia		South & Central America	E/T	Su	Lavender or lilac with white or yellow blotch	35
U. violacea	violet bladderwort	Australia	T	Te	Violet with yellow	10
U. viscosa		C & S America (N)	T	Su	Violet with yellow spot	50
U. vitellina		Malaysia	T	Tr	Yellow with brown	5
U. vulgaris		Europe, North Africa, Asia	A	Te	Yellow with reddish brown streaks	25
U. warburgii		China	T	Te	Bluish-purple	10
U. warmingii		Venezuela, Brazil, Bolivia	A	Su	Yellow	5
U. welwitschii		Tropical Africa, Madagascar	T	Tr	Violet or mauve with yellow blotch	50
U. westonii		West Australia	T	Te	Pink with darker pink spots	25
U. wightiana		India	T	Su	Violet	40

Bibliography

Albert, V., Williams, S. and Chase, M., 'Carnivorous Plants: Phylogeny and Structural Evolution', *Science*, Vol. 257, 1992

Carnivorous Plant Newsletter, Official Journal of the International Carnivorous Plant Society, 1990–1997

Cheers, G., *A Guide to Carnivorous Plants of the World*, Collins Angus and Robertson Publishers, New South Wales, 1992

Danser, B.H., 'The Nepenthaceae of the Netherlands Indies', *Bulletin de Buitenzorg*, Series III, Vol. IX, 249–438, 1929

Darwin, C., *Insectivorous Plants*, London, John Murray, 1876

Elliot, R. and Jones, D., *Encyclopedia of Australian Plants*, Volume 3, Lothian Publishing company, 1984

Environment, Volume 36 Number 4

Erickson, E., *Plants of Prey*, Lamb Publications, Osborne Park, Western Australia, 1968

Jebb, M. and Cheek, M., 'A skeletal revision of Nepenthes', *Blumea 42*, Rijksherbrium/Hortus Botanicus, The Netherlands, 1997

Lecloufe, M., *Carnivorous Plants*, Blandford, London, 1990

Lowrie, A., *Carnivorous Plants of Australia*, Volume 1 and 2, University of Western Australia Press, Western Australia, 1987 & 1989

Mason, John, *Yates Guide to Pests and Diseases*, Angus and Robertson, 1995

Moore, R., *Charles Darwin, A Great Life in Brief*, Alfred A Knopf, 1955

Nuytsia, Bulletin of Western Australian Herbarium, Volumes 8, 9, 10 & 11, 1992, 1994, 1996

Phillips, A. and Lamb, A., *Pitcher Plants of Borneo*, Natural History Publications, Malaysia, 1996

Pietropaolo, J. & P., *Carnivorous Plants of the World*, Timber Press, Oregon, 1986

Schlauer, J., Jan Schlauer's nomenclature synopsis, 1995

Slack, A., *Carnivorous Plants*, Ebury Press, London, 1979

Slack, A., *Insect Eating Plants and How to Grow Them*, Alphabooks, England, 1986

Taylor, P., 'The Genus Utricularia' a taxanomic monograph, Her Majesty's Stationery Office, London, 1989

Victorian Carnivorous Plant Society, Carnivorous Plants Total Listing, VCPS, 1995

Victorian Carnivorous Plant Society. Various journals, 1985–1997

Walker, R., *The genus* Pinguicula*, Pings: Care and Cultivation*, 1996

Index

Illustrations are indicated by italic type.